THE DAILY STUDY BIBLE

(OLD TESTAMENT)

General Editor: John C. L. Gibson

ECCLESIASTES
and SONG OF SOLOMON

ECCLESIASTES
and
SONG OF SOLOMON

ROBERT DAVIDSON

THE SAINT ANDREW PRESS
EDINBURGH

THE WESTMINSTER PRESS
PHILADELPHIA

Published by
The Saint Andrew Press
Edinburgh, Scotland
and
The Westminster Press®
Philadelphia, Pennsylvania

British Library Cataloguing in Publication Data
Davidson, Robert
 Ecclesiastes and Song of Solomon.—(The Daily Study Bible)
 1. Bible. O.T. Ecclesiastes—Commentaries
 2. Bible. O.T. Song of Solomon—Commentaries
 I. Title II. Bible. O.T. Ecclesiastes.
 English. Revised Standard. 1986
 III. Bible. O.T. Song of Solomon.
 English. Revised Standard. 1986
 IV. Series
 223'.8077 BS1475.3

ISBN 0-7152-0537-4

Printed and bound in Great Britain
by Thomson Litho Ltd., East Kilbride, Scotland

ISBN (Great Britain) 07152 0537 4

GENERAL PREFACE

This series of commentaries on the Old Testament, to which the present volume on *Ecclesiastes and Song of Solomon* belongs, has been planned as a companion series to the much-acclaimed New Testament series of the late Professor William Barclay. As with that series, each volume is arranged in successive headed portions suitable for daily study. The Biblical text followed is that of the Revised Standard Version or Common Bible. Eleven contributors share the work, each being responsible for from one to three volumes. The series is issued in the hope that it will do for the Old Testament what Professor Barclay's series succeeded so splendidly in doing for the New Testament—make it come alive for the Christian believer in the twentieth century.

Its two-fold aim is the same as his. Firstly, it is intended to introduce the reader to some of the more important results and fascinating insights of modern Old Testament scholarship. Most of the contributors are already established experts in the field with many publications to their credit. Some are younger scholars who have yet to make their names but who in my judgment as General Editor are now ready to be tested. I can assure those who use these commentaries that they are in the hands of competent teachers who know what is of real consequence in their subject and are able to present it in a form that will appeal to the general public.

The primary purpose of the series, however, is *not* an academic one. Professor Barclay summed it up for his New Testament series in the words of Richard of Chichester's prayer—to enable men and women "to know Jesus Christ more clearly, to love Him more dearly, and to follow Him more nearly." In the case of the Old Testament we have to be a little more circumspect than that. The Old Testament was completed long before the time of Our Lord, and it was (as it still is) the sole Bible of the Jews, God's first people, before it became part of the Christian Bible. We must take this fact seriously.

Yet in its strangely compelling way, sometimes dimly and sometimes directly, sometimes charmingly and sometimes embarrassingly, it holds up before us the things of Christ. It should not be forgotten that Jesus Himself was raised on this Book, that He based His whole ministry on what it says, and that He approached His death with its words on His lips. Christian men and women have in this ancient collection of Jewish writings a uniquely illuminating avenue not only into the will and purposes of God the Father, but into the mind and heart of Him who is named God's Son, who was Himself born a Jew but went on through the Cross and Resurrection to become the Saviour of the world. Read reverently and imaginatively the Old Testament can become a living and relevant force in their everyday lives.

It is the prayer of myself and my colleagues that this series may be used by its readers and blessed by God to that end.

New College　　　　　　　　　　　JOHN C. L. GIBSON
Edinburgh　　　　　　　　　　　　　　General Editor

CONTENTS

INTRODUCTION

The two books that we are going to study in this volume have certain things in common. Like another Old Testament book—Proverbs—and a book that was not accepted into the Jewish Bible—the Wisdom of Solomon—they are linked in tradition to King Solomon, the patron saint of 'wisdom' in ancient Israel. They are both, moreover, puzzling books which from early times have raised many an eyebrow: Song of Solomon, because it was a favourite in the 'banqueting houses' when the assembled male company was suitably relaxed and mellow; Ecclesiastes, because it was full of contradictions and seemed to have a rather jaundiced view of life.

One of the Jewish Rabbis argued that Solomon wrote three Old Testament books in the following order: Song of Songs (he uses its Hebrew title) first, Proverbs second and Ecclesiastes last, because, "When a man is young he sings songs. When he becomes an adult he utters practical proverbs. When he becomes old he voices the vanity of things". No doubt there are people who sing their way through the ardour and passion of youth, come to a practical and common sense maturity, and end up disillusioned. Neither Ecclesiastes nor Song of Solomon, however, make any sense if both are considered as coming from the pen of Solomon. The books are far too different, not only in thought but in language and style, for them to have the same author. It would be as easy to argue that the poems of Robert Burns were written by Oscar Wilde.

We may, however, be glad that they were linked in tradition to Solomon, otherwise it is doubtful whether they would have made it into the scriptures which we call the Old Testament. If they had not, then that would have been our loss, because they are both fascinating, surprising and, in some ways, challenging and disturbing books. To appreciate them and to learn from them, you may have to begin by laying aside many of the ideas you may have as to what a 'religious' book ought to offer you. Here you will look in vain for a clear statement of accepted religious beliefs; nor will you find yourself borne along on the wings of untroubled certainties. But you will find a refreshing honesty and a healthy exploration of the most powerful of human emotions, presented to us in the conviction that all of life, its unanswered questions and its passions, its joys and its frustrations, come to us from God.

ECCLESIASTES

INTRODUCTION

Of no book of the Bible is it more true than of Ecclesiastes that people have tended to read into it what they want to hear, and to get out of it what agrees with their own prejudices and convictions. Thus in the fourth century A.D. Jerome used the book to encourage a Roman lady of his acquaintance to renounce the things of this world. The book's purpose, he claimed, is "to show the utter vanity of every earthly enjoyment and hence the necessity of betaking oneself to an ascetic life, devoted entirely to the service of God". If you wonder how he got round the verses in the book which urge that a man should "eat and drink and find enjoyment in his toil" (*eg* 2:24), it was by interpreting such passages as an invitation to participate in the sacrament of the Eucharist or the Lord's Supper. In the sixteenth century, Martin Luther on the contrary found the book to be world affirming: "The design of the book," he claimed, "is to teach us to use with grateful hearts the things present and the creatures which are bountifully bestowed upon us by God, without anxiety about future temporal blessings". More recently there are those who have found in the book "the smell of the tomb" or "the joy of life". Just over a hundred years ago a comprehensive survey of the various ways in which the book had been interpreted by Jewish and Christian scholars across the centuries concluded with the words, "What a solemn lesson for the pious and the learned to abstain from dogmatism, and what an admonition not to urge one's own pious emotions or ingenious conceits as the Word of God!". Of course the man who wrote these words of warning fell into the same trap, and others have been doing it ever since. It is always easy to see how others do it, but not so easy to see that we may be in the same boat.

3

There is a further problem. Hebrew, unlike English, makes no use of quotation marks, so there are places in the book where we are not sure whether we are listening to the writer's own views or whether he is quoting and commenting on the views of others. What we think he is doing can make a great difference to the meaning of a passage. Turn for a moment to 2:13–14. The RSV translation reads: "Then I saw that wisdom excels folly as light excels darkness. The wise man has his eyes in his head, but the fool walks in darkness; and yet I perceived that one fate comes to all of them". Here then is a considered statement by the writer of the book, that in this present life there are real advantages in being wise rather than in being a fool; at the end of the day, however, whether you are wise or a fool, you come to the same fate—death. That is also the view taken by the New English Bible. But turn to the Good News Bible and we read: "Oh, I know, 'Wisdom is better than foolishness, just as light is better than darkness. Wise men can see where they are going, and fools cannot.' But I also know that the same fate is waiting for us all." In this case the writer of the book is either quoting a widely accepted view and saying to us, 'Yes, that may very well be right, but never forget ...'; or the "Oh, I know" at the beginning is sarcastic and the writer is saying, 'Don't believe this for a moment, no matter how often you may have heard it: the one certain fact in life for all of us, wise and foolish alike, is death'. Which translation, which particular emphasis is right? We do not know. Much depends on the overall picture we have in our minds of the author of the book. Perhaps the best thing you can do now is to sit down and read through the book from beginning to end. It will not take you long. Try to build up your own picture of the man behind the words and see how many of the bits and pieces in the book you can fit together. All this Daily Study Bible commentary can offer you is one such picture, with no claim being made that it is the only possible picture.

If you read through the book carefully you may find yourself becoming puzzled. You certainly ought to be puzzled if you have any feeling for the faith and the certainties so finely expressed in many other parts of the Old Testament. A Psalmist (see *eg*

Ps. 136) will look out on the world of creation all around him and marvel; he will think of what God has done for his people in the past and will give voice to a hymn of praise and thanksgiving for that "steadfast love" that undergirds all life. The author of Ecclesiastes looks out on the same world, the generations that come and go, the sun, the wind, the rivers flowing to the sea, and comes to the conclusion that it is an unending, meaningless, monotonous round; "there is nothing new under the sun" (1:9). The prophets of Israel look out on an unjust, corrupt society and demand, in the name of God, repentance and a new order of society that will reflect God's concern for "justice" and "righteousness" (*eg* Amos 5:24). This man looks out on the same kind of society, shrugs his shoulders and says, 'It's the system, you can't beat it' (*eg* Eccles. 5:8).

Here we need to keep in mind two things:

(a) The Book of Ecclesiastes is one of the latest books in the Old Testament. Although the author is introduced in 1:1 as "the son of David, king in Jerusalem", the book was not written by Solomon in the tenth century B.C. Language alone is decisive at this point; it has clear links with Aramaic and post-biblical Hebrew. To claim that it is written by Solomon is like saying, as one scholar has put it, that "a book about Marxism in modern English idiom and spelling was written by Henry VIII". We have got to come down to the third century B.C. at the earliest before this book makes sense. Behind it there lie many, if not most, of the other books in the Old Testament.

(b) The author of the book was well aware, as we shall see, of the traditional faith and religious teaching that had shaped his people's life. Such things, however, no longer seem to ring bells for him. Somewhere along the line the answers he had been taught no longer satisfied him. He takes a long cool look at life and experience as it comes to him, and reaches very different conclusions. Some of his comments are so sharp and provocative that many scholars believe that what he wrote has been toned down and made more acceptable to more conventional religious minds by the addition of verses like 12:13: "Fear God, and keep his commandments; for this is the whole duty of man". We shall discuss this view as we go along. Certainly this is a man who puts a large question mark against many things that others believed. In this he is, perhaps, close to many people today who are brought up in the Church, brought up to accept traditional Christian teaching, yet who find that neither the Church nor that teaching any longer make much sense to them.

If, of course, you come out attacking or questioning people's deeply held beliefs, you are not likely to be popular. What this man said seems to have caused offence right from the beginning. Towards the end of the book a friend or disciple tries to defend him. He sought, claims this friend, "to find pleasing words, and uprightly he wrote words of truth" (12:10). And if you find some of the things he says hurtful or upsetting, remember that that is what God's truth often is: "The sayings of the wise are like goads, and like nails firmly fixed are the collected sayings which are given by one Shepherd" (12:11).

We have spoken so far of "this man", or the writer or author of Ecclesiastes: but who was he and what do we know about him? To find answers to these questions we must turn to the book.

A MAN AND HIS THEME SONG—I

Ecclesiastes 1:1–2

> ¹The words of the Preacher, the
>   son of David, king in Jerusalem.
> ²Vanity of vanities, says the Preacher,
>   vanity of vanities! All is vanity.

"The words of the Preacher": "Preacher" is a translation of the Hebrew word *Koheleth*—see RSV footnote—which we owe to Martin Luther. It is not a very happy translation. Few congregations would put up with this preacher for very long in the pulpit. Other modern translations go for "the Philosopher" (GNB), "the Speaker" (NEB) or "the President": thus the opening phrase would be a reasonable Hebrew equivalent to "The Thoughts of Chairman Mao". We shall stick from now on to the Hebrew word *Koheleth,* since there is perhaps no one English word which exactly conveys its meaning. It is a word related to the Hebrew word *kahal,* a 'gathering' or 'assembly', very often an assembly of the people for worship and instruction. This word *kahal* is rendered in the Greek Old Testament by the Greek word *ecclesia*; hence "Ecclesiastes", as a translation of Koheleth, and the name which we normally give to the book. It is from this same Greek word, of course, that we get our English word 'ecclesiastical'. Koheleth may very well mean someone who holds a particular office or who has a particular function in a *kahal.* Koheleth is therefore not this man's personal name. We only know him by his title, as if we were to speak all the time simply of 'Mr President' or 'the Prime Minister'.

But what kind of gathering or assembly was this in which he functioned? There is so much in the book about Wisdom—the search for wisdom, the value and limitations of wisdom, so many passages that contain typical wisdom sayings like those we find in Proverbs—that it is best to think of him as one of the learned wise men whose thoughts, teaching and advice on everyday problems and on the affairs of state were valued in ancient Israel. Such a man, who had a reputation for wisdom, would gather round him a group of people anxious to learn from him. So Koheleth is a kind of teacher in a wisdom school. Perhaps we might think of him today as a university Professor or Lecturer—Professor Wise?— and like many other Professors, not least those in theology, his views could be sometimes upsetting. The description of this man as "the son of David, king in Jerusalem", taken together with the words of 1:12—"I . . . have been king over Israel in Jerusalem"— may have been intended to provide a link with Solomon, the royal patron of wisdom. As we have seen, this is impossible. Koheleth lived many centuries after Solomon. The words may, however, indicate that here is a man accustomed to moving in high society. It was at court and under the auspices of the king that the wise men came into their own in Israel. As advisors to the king on matters of state, they were like 'Privy Counsellors' or the White House Staff. The words translated "king" may indeed mean simply 'counsellor'. Everything else in the book points to a man who is essentially artistocratic in out-look, conservative in his tastes, with wealth enough to get whatever good things in life take his fancy.

We are moving here in a different world from much of that which we find elsewhere in the Old Testament. The sense of identity with the poor, the championing of the cause of the victims of social change, which are such marked features of the teaching of many of the Old Testament prophets, are here entirely lacking. Nor does he claim, like a prophet, to be giving us "the word of the Lord". The book begins, like some of the prophetic books, with the phrase "the words of X"; but in the case of a prophetic book, *eg* Jeremiah, this opening is further explained by a phrase such as "to whom the word of the Lord came". There is no such claim here; only "the words of Koheleth", his own opinions, his own comments and observations on life. But such observations and comments may be just as challenging and provocative as the words of one who claims to be giving voice to "the word of the Lord". There are those today unmoved by many a sermon claiming to proclaim "the word of the Lord" to them, yet who are arrested and challenged by the words of a C. S. Lewis or of a David Jenkins, Bishop of Durham.

A MAN AND HIS THEME SONG—II

Ecclesiastes 1:1–2 (*cont'd*)

Just as certain TV programmes can be immediately identified by their theme music, just as the opening bars of Beethoven's fifth symphony spelled out the V for Victory message to occupied Europe in the dark days from 1940 onwards, so there is one phrase forever associated with Koheleth: "Vanity of vanities ... vanity of vanities! All is vanity" (1:2), words which in one form or another echo across the book from beginning to end.

But what do they mean? Modern English translations, unless they stick to "vanity of vanities", offer us a wide variety of interpretations. "It is useless, useless ... life is useless, all useless," says the Good News Bible; "Emptiness, emptiness ... all is empty," says the New English Bible; "Meaningless, meaningless

... utterly meaningless," says the New International Version. Let us take a closer look at the Hebrew word translated "vanity". It is the word *hebel,* whose basic meaning seems to be 'breath' or 'vapour'. Always it points to something which is insubstantial or transitory or in some sense futile. It is frequently used in the Old Testament to describe the gods of other people, powerless idols (*eg* Jer. 8:19; 10:8). It can refer to any activity which seems to be pointless. There is, however, no other writer in the Old Testament who takes a look at the whole of life, all human experience, and sums it up in the words "vanity of vanities". Just as in Hebrew, "king of kings" means the greatest king, and "slave of slaves" the meanest slave, so this expression is a way of saying 'it is all completely *hebel*'. There seems to be no point or purpose in life.

We must not misunderstand what Koheleth is saying here. This does not mean that he finds life uninteresting. Far from it; he is fascinated by life and its curious twists and turns. It does not mean that he does not enjoy life. He gets a great deal of enjoyment out of life. What he *is* saying is that when you take a long hard look at life, you must place beside it a large question mark. It just does not add up. It does not make sense; it is empty of any ultimate meaning. While other voices in the Old Testament may speak with assured certainty about the meaning of life, Koheleth cannot and does not. While others claim to know the will of God, God's purposes for him remain an insoluble puzzle.

At this point he stands alongside many people today; good people who have been brought up in a tradition of faith, but for whom many of the ancient certainties no longer make sense. They are people who enjoy life, who get a lot out of it and give a lot to it, but who when pressed can only say, 'I don't know what it all means'. We may seek to meet their perplexities with our certainties, we may try to replace their 'no answers' with our answers. We might be better advised at times to direct them to this interesting fellow traveller in the Bible, who may have something to say to them as they share his journey. Perhaps if we are honest we shall all find something of ourselves in him.

WHAT'S THE POINT?

Ecclesiastes 1:3–11

3 What does man gain by all the toil
    at which he toils under the sun?
4 A generation goes, and a generation comes,
    but the earth remains for ever.
5 The sun rises and the sun goes down,
    and hastens to the place where it rises.
6 The wind blows to the south,
    and goes round to the north;
 round and round goes the wind,
    and on its circuits the wind returns.
7 All streams run to the sea,
    but the sea is not full;
 to the place where the streams flow,
    there they flow again.
8 All things are full of weariness;
    a man cannot utter it;
 the eye is not satisfied with seeing,
    nor the ear filled with hearing.
9 What has been is what will be,
    and what has been done is what will be done;
    and there is nothing new under the sun.
10 Is there a thing of which it is said,
    "See, this is new"?
 It has been already,
    in the ages before us.
11 There is no remembrance of former things,
    nor will there be any remembrance
 of later things yet to happen
    among those who come after.

Koheleth now begins to develop his basic theme. You put a lot of trouble and effort into life, says Koheleth—the word translated "toil" in verse 3 is a favourite word of his and can mean either hard work or the reward you get for such work— but what is the point, what dividends does it pay? We are here today and gone tomorrow in a world that goes on and on and on. The sun rises, the sun sets, and tomorrow it begins all over again. The wind may change direction, but soon it will veer round to blow in the same direction as it did yesterday or the day before yesterday. The rivers keep on pouring their waters into the sea, but does it make any difference to the sea? On and on, over and over again, a picture of that weary monotony that is life. In the face of it, men are reduced to silence and no human experience can ever be fully satisfying (v. 8). Neither the present nor the future can contain any surprises. We can only say 'we have been here before'; "there is nothing new under the sun" (v. 9). If people claim otherwise it is only because they have short memories. They have no greater information about what happened in the past than future generations will have about what is happening now.

This may all sound fairly depressing, the jaundiced view of a man for whom life has just gone flat. Maybe it is, but there is more to it than that; more that ought to make us stop and think.

(a) There are features of life that are simply there, things we must come to terms with in one way or another. The generations do 'come and go'. None of us are issued with an ever renewable season ticket for this life. The world was there before we took our first unsteady steps upon it, and it is likely still to be there when we have taken our last faltering steps. Sometimes we feel like pioneers exploring virgin territory only to discover the footprints of those who have travelled this way before us. How to come to terms with this, the frailty and the transitoriness of human life, is a question to which we shall find Koheleth returning again and again.

(b) There is a saying that 'one man's fish can be another man's poison'! The same steady beat of the created world, sun, wind and river, which speaks to a Psalmist of the glory of God and leads him to a joyous celebration of the praise of God (*eg* Ps. 104), speaks to Koheleth only of a soulless machine, programmed robot-like. This is what life can seem like for many people, with today but yesterday all over again with its pressing problems, and tomorrow promising to be no different. Meanwhile all around are people using all the tricks of high powered advertizing to convince us that they have something 'new' to offer; from that 'new' biological soap powder which does not really get the dirt out of the jeans any more effectively, or that 'new' glossy weekly magazine which turns out to be not all that different from others on the market, to the claims of Scientology and countless other 'ologies', pretending to offer us something 'new'. There is a healthy dose of disbelief that we need to bring to many of the claims for the 'new' with which we are being continuously bombarded. It is one of the marks of Koheleth that he is not prepared to swallow what other people say or claim, just because they say it. He refuses to be taken for a ride. To every claim he says, 'show me how it works out in life or don't expect me to accept it'. It is a fair question to ask about every claim that we make for our faith.

THE STRANGE DIVIDEND OF WISDOM

Ecclesiastes 1:12–18

[12]I the Preacher have been king over Israel in Jerusalem. [13]And I applied my mind to seek and to search out by wisdom all that is done under heaven; it is an unhappy business that God has given to the sons of men to be busy with. [14]I have seen everything that is done under the sun; and behold, all is vanity and a striving after wind.

[15]What is crooked cannot be made straight,
　　and what is lacking cannot be numbered.

[16]I said to myself, "I have acquired great wisdom, surpassing all who were over Jerusalem before me; and my mind has had great experience of wisdom and knowledge." [17]And I applied my mind to know wisdom and to know madness and folly. I perceived that this also is but a striving after wind.

[18]For in much wisdom is much vexation,
　　and he who increases knowledge increases sorrow.

Koheleth, as we have seen, belongs to the ranks of 'the wise men' in Israel. They had a two-fold role: (1) to observe human conduct and to give practical advice on how to live the good and the successful life, and (2) to lay bare the basic principles on which the good and the successful life functions. For many of the wisdom teachers this meant drawing attention to the fundamental religious basis of all true wisdom: "the fear of the Lord is the beginning of knowledge" (Prov. 1:7).

This wise man invites us to join him in a voyage of exploration, to take a close look at all that goes on in this world in which our lives are set. Like many other voyages of discovery, it takes him and us into strange regions where many of the familiar landmarks are missing. Don't sign on for this voyage unless you are willing to leave the well-beaten tracks. The attempt to make sense of life, says Koheleth, is "an unhappy business" (v. 13), or to use a Scottish expression, 'it's a gie sair fecht'. It is *hebel* (see above) and a 'striving after wind' (v. 14), a favourite phrase of this writer and one which occurs nowhere else in the Old Testament. Life, he says to us, has a kind of will-o'-the-wisp quality about it. You may think at one moment that you are catching up with it, that you have got it, only to discover at the next moment that it has slipped through your fingers. It cannot be pinned down. Here is a sensitive modern artiste saying in her own way much the same thing: "If I have learned anything it is that life forms no logical patterns. It is haphazard and full of beauties which I try to catch as they fly by, for who knows whether any of them will ever return?" (Margot Fonteyn, *Autobiography* p. 272). This 'who knows?' and the questioning shrug of the shoulders, we shall meet with again and again as we journey with Koheleth. Two factors influence his attitude:

(a) He believes that there are many things in life over which we have no control, things that we cannot change, no matter how hard we may wish to change them: "You can't straighten out what is crooked; you can't count things that aren't there" (v. 15 GNB). He is not thinking here about the kind of people we are—we all know how difficult it is to change our attitudes. He is thinking about the world in which we live. As he says in 7:13, "Consider the work of God; who can make straight what he has made crooked?" At this point he is miles away from the prophets in the Old Testament who will look at what is crooked in society around them and demand in the name of God that it be put right. There was revolution in their thoughts. In Koheleth's mind there is only acceptance, even in the face of what is twisted and perverse. That is the way God has made it, he says, and there is nothing we can do about it. Perhaps we need a greater wisdom, the wisdom expressed in the words of a prayer:

> God grant me the serenity to accept the things I cannot change,
> the courage to change the things I can,
> and the wisdom to know the difference.

(b) The further he explores, the deeper he digs, the greater his problem becomes. Increasing knowledge only brings increasing sorrow (v. 18). We must not misunderstand him. He is not advocating a simple faith that asks no questions. He believes that we have got to ask questions; that it is important to look searchingly at life so that we know the difference between what leads to the good and successful life and what is sheer stupidity and folly. He has no time for the unthinking fool. Yet the further he explores, the more uncertain his journey becomes. In the end, he is left facing a mystery which he is no nearer solving than when he set out. For all his knowledge, he is no nearer discovering the ultimate meaning of life. It is refreshing to meet a man who is so honest about the limitations of his own knowledge. There is little comfort here for anyone who believes that all that we need to solve the problems of the world and to unlock the riddle of the universe is a little, or a lot, more knowledge.

THE PURSUIT OF PLEASURE?

Ecclesiastes 2:1–11

[1]I said to myself, "Come now, I will make a test of pleasure; enjoy yourself." But behold, this also was vanity. [2]I said of laughter, "It is mad," and of pleasure, "What use is it?" [3]I searched with my mind how to cheer my body with wine—my mind still guiding me with wisdom—and how to lay hold on folly, till I might see what was good for the sons of men to do under heaven during the few days of their life. [4]I made great works; I built houses and planted vineyards for myself; [5]I made myself gardens and parks, and planted in them all kinds of fruit trees. [6]I made myself pools from which to water the forest of growing

trees. ⁷I bought male and female slaves, and had slaves who were born in my house; I had also great possessions of herds and flocks, more than any who had been before me in Jerusalem. ⁸I also gathered for myself silver and gold and the treasure of kings and provinces; I got singers, both men and women, and many concubines, man's delight.

⁹ So I became great and surpassed all who were before me in Jerusalem; also my wisdom remained with me. ¹⁰And whatever my eyes desired I did not keep from them; I kept my heart from no pleasure, for my heart found pleasure in all my toil, and this was my reward for all my toil. ¹¹Then I considered all that my hands had done and the toil I had spent on doing it, and behold, all was vanity and a striving after wind, and there was nothing to be gained under the sun.

Give Koheleth his due; he is not easily put off. If knowledge does not provide the answer to where the true meaning of life is to be found, what does? Why not try the pursuit of pleasure? Before we dismissively lump him together with the pleasure-seeking crowds of today or of any day, let us notice what he is doing. He is *not* advocating mindless debauchery. You would never have found him drunk and incapable or among the helpless heroin addicts. In all that he does he is determined to remain in self-control—"my mind still guiding me with wisdom" (v. 3). He would seek the stimulus of wine, yes, but never be its victim. This is an experiment. He wants to see whether it works. It does not. Like many a person before and after him, he discovers that the pursuit of pleasure, the search for happiness, is self-defeating.

He lived it up in great style. He built for himself his own secure world, with all the marks of what we normally consider worldly success. No doubt if he were alive today he would be in oil, or be the chairman of a large international company. He would have his villas in Switzerland and in the Bahamas, as well as a penthouse in London and in New York. He was a patron of the arts. He gratified his sexual desires. He was a liberated self-made man with every reason to be proud of his achievements. And the verdict? It meant nothing, all so much *hebel,* so much "striving after wind" (v. 11). It is not that he has any regrets about his life style; he does not apologize for it. It merely confirmed for him that the pursuit of pleasure was not the answer to the ultimate questions of life. The fact that he found no answer in the equivalent of the private jet and the 'Dynasty' life style, should make us stop and question our sense of values. Is life really about keeping up with, or out-Jonesing, the Joneses? Koheleth, like all of us, needed to be faced with the challenge in the paradoxical words of Jesus: ". . . whoever would save his life will lose it; and whoever loses his life for my sake, he will save it. For what does it profit a man if he gains the whole world and loses or forfeits himself?" (Luke 9:24–25). Koheleth set out to gain all the world had to offer; but he never found himself.

FLIES IN THE OINTMENT

Ecclesiastes 2:12–23

12So I turned to consider wisdom and madness and folly; for what can the man do who comes after the king? Only what he has already done. 13Then I saw that wisdom excels folly as light excels darkness. 14The wise man has his eyes in his head, but the fool walks in darkness; and yet I perceived that one fate comes to all of them. 15Then I said to myself, "What befalls the fool will befall me also; why then have I been so very wise?" And I said to myself that this also is vanity. 16For of the wise man as of the fool there is no enduring remembrance, seeing that in the days to come all will have been long forgotten. How the wise man dies just like the fool! 17So I hated life, because what is done under the sun was grievous to me; for all is vanity and a striving after wind.

18I hated all my toil in which I had toiled under the sun, seeing that I must leave it to the man who will come after me; 19and who knows whether he will be a wise man or a fool? Yet he will be master of all for which I toiled and used my wisdom under the sun. This also is vanity. 20So I turned about and gave my heart up to despair over all the toil of my labours under the sun, 21because sometimes a man who has toiled with wisdom and knowledge and skill must leave all to be enjoyed by a man who did not toil for it. This also is vanity and a great evil. 22What has a man from all the toil and strain with which he toils beneath the sun? 23For all his days are full of pain, and his work is a vexation; even in the night his mind does not rest. This also is vanity.

The pursuit of pleasure having led only to a dead end, Koheleth warns that if he, with all the resources at his disposal, found it to be like that, it is hardly likely to turn out any differently for anyone else—this seems to be the meaning of the difficult second half of verse 12 for which our English Bibles offer a wide variety of interpretations. He turns, therefore, to look at human experience in all its rich variety, from 'wisdom' at one end of the spectrum to 'folly' at the other. We have already discussed various interpretations of verses 13–14 in the Introduction (p. 4). Yes, he says, there is practical value in wisdom; it can guide you through life and prevent you from making many a stupid mistake. But there are two snags:

(a) In the long run, whether you are wise or a fool you share the same fate (vv. 15–17). You come face to face with death, death that makes a mockery of so many of our human pretentions, desires and achievements. This is a thought that is never far from Koheleth's mind. He knows that he will stand one day, like all of us, at the last frontier; and beyond it, for him, there is only a great unknown (cf. 3:19–21). Once he has stepped beyond that frontier, whatever his reputation may have been, he will soon be forgotten. Like most of the voices that come to us from the Old Testament he has no assurance of any other life. He does not know that death has lost its sting, swallowed up in the victory of our Risen Lord (1 Cor. 15:54ff.). He is closer to the mood so well expressed in Rupert Brooke's poem:

Oh Death will find me, long before I tire
    Of watching you; and swing me suddenly
Into the shade and loneliness and mire
    Of the last stand.

Koheleth knows he must accept this fact; but he does not do so without protest. Most of our English translations of verse 16 suggest that the mood is one of regret or resignation. Thus the New English Bible translates, "Alas, wise man and fool die the same death!" It is better to hear in these words a cry of protest as well as anguish—"How *can* the wise man die just like the fool?"—a protest against something which Koheleth finds hard to come to terms with. It is all wrong, says Koheleth. Why should all the distinctions that mean so much to us in life, the distinction, for example, between a wise man and a fool, suddenly mean nothing when we come face to face with the one certainty in life for all of us?

(b) There is another wrong that rankles (vv. 18–23). You may use all your skill, your ability, your energy; you may work yourself to the bone, burn the midnight oil to carve out for yourself a secure future ... and then death strikes. All that you have so strenuously worked for then passes to someone else, who has not lifted a finger to earn it, who may have none of your ability and dedication, who may be nothing other than a fool. It is not a comforting thought; it is "a great evil" (v. 21), all part of that unanswerable 'why?' that lurks at the centre of life.

Koheleth thinks ... and it hurts. He is too honest for it not to hurt.

COMING TO TERMS WITH LIFE

Ecclesiastes 2:24–26

²⁴There is nothing better for a man than that he should eat and drink, and find enjoyment in his toil. This also, I saw, is from the hand of God; ²⁵for apart from him who can eat or who can have enjoyment? ²⁶For to the man who pleases him God gives wisdom and knowledge and joy; but to the sinner he gives the work of gathering and heaping, only to give to one who pleases God. This also is vanity and a striving after wind.

How then does Koheleth come to terms with the undeniable and hurting facts of life? In this passage we hear for the first time his positive advice, advice which he is to repeat in one way or another throughout the book: there is nothing better for a man than that he should eat and drink and find enjoyment in his toil (v. 24; cf. 3:12–13; 5:18; 8:15; 9:7).

What is he inviting us to do? To go on enjoying ourselves because nothing else matters? No! Or to accept the basic things of life, such as food and drink, as being good in themselves? No, not simply that.

We have got to set these words against the background of all the other things he has been saying. There are, he claims, no answers to the deepest questions in life. God does not want us to tear our hair out looking for such answers. He has given us life, that is all, and our responsibility is to live it to the full as it comes to us day by day, asking no unnecessary questions. It is our ordinary, God-given life that is important, not our thoughts about it.

It is an age-old philosophy. We hear it on the lips of an inn-keeper in the ancient Babylonian tale of Gilgamesh. When she is informed that Gilgamesh is trying to discover the secret of eternal life, she says to him:

> The life you seek you shall not find.
> When the gods created mankind,
> Death for mankind they set aside,
> Life in their own hands retaining.
> Gilgamesh, fill your belly,
> Enjoy yourself by day and by night.
> . . . .
> Pay attention to the little one who holds on to your hand,
> Let your wife find delight in your arms.
> For this is the task of mankind.

It is also a modern philosophy. Listen again to Dame Margot Fonteyn: "The important thing is to live, laugh, suffer, eat and love and let the rest take care of itself" (op. cit., p. 206). It is the common sense attitude of many people. Preachers may insist that people must be concerned about the big and ultimate issues in life, but many people are not. They are prepared to settle for life as it comes to them, take the rough with the smooth, and live it to the best of their ability. Such a one was Koheleth. He reached this conclusion not because he had not thought about life, but because he *had* thought about it, long and hard, and had come to the conclusion that no other attitude made sense. He does not settle for this as a second best; he believes that this is what God wants from him, it comes "from the hand of God" (v. 24). Although verse 25 is difficult and may be translated in various ways, it seems to be stressing the same point. We may not agree with him, but we should respect his integrity. He is not prepared to make larger claims about life than he can defend.

Interestingly, much the same thing is said about death and life by another Jewish writer, Jesus the son of Sirach, the author of the book in the Apocrypha which we call Ecclesiasticus; and he says it from within the context of a much warmer, more assured and traditional faith (Ecclesiasticus 14:12–17):

> Remember that death is not to be postponed;
> the hour of your appointment with the grave is undisclosed.
> Before you die, do good to your friend;
> reach out as far as you can to help him.
> Do not miss a day's enjoyment
> or forgo your share of innocent pleasure.
> Are you to leave to others all you have laboured for
> and let them draw lots for your hard-earned wealth?
> Give and receive; indulge yourself;
> you need not expect luxuries in the grave.
> Man's body wears out like a garment;
> for the ancient sentence stands: You shall die.

Whether we say this like Jesus the son of Sirach within the security of a traditional faith, or like Koheleth, vulnerable and living with many unanswered questions, we are being reminded of what we all share; life as it comes to us day by day, life which we are called upon to handle responsibly and to accept gladly as God's gift to us. And if we don't do that we won't get very far in any pilgrimage of faith.

Verse 26 is an interesting example of the problems we face when we try to enter into Koheleth's mind. If we think that behind all Koheleth's questions there is a man who remains firm in the faith of his fathers, or if we think of him as a man who expresses and enters into the doubts of other people in order to help them through to a more certain faith, then we can read this verse as expressing such a faith. Remember, he says, the man who pleases God receives rich and satisfying gifts, spiritual gifts— "wisdom and knowledge and joy"— but the man who rejects God—"the sinner"—struggles to amass the things of this world, things which he cannot keep. If, however, we see Koheleth, as this commentary does, as a man trying to come to terms with his own doubts, a man who has serious reservations about the faith in which he has been brought up, then we can read this verse very differently.

Look at life, he says: it is just a fact that some people seem to get a lot more out of it than others. The first group must be those who "please" and are acceptable to God, while the others just fail to make the grade; the word translated "sinners" coming from a verb which means to miss the mark. Why and how God divides people into these different categories remains one of the unsolved mysteries of life (cf. 9:1–2). Perhaps this should remind us not to be too quick or certain in our judgments of people. The standards that we apply may not be God's standards. In the great parable of judgment in Matthew 25:31–46, both the sheep and the goats are surprised to find themselves where they are.

THE RICH AND PUZZLING TAPESTRY OF LIFE

Ecclesiastes 3:1–15

[1]For everything there is a season,
 and a time for every matter under heaven:
[2]a time to be born, and a time to die;
 a time to plant, and a time to pluck up what is planted;
[3]a time to kill, and a time to heal;
 a time to break down, and a time to build up;
[4]a time to weep, and a time to laugh;
 a time to mourn, and a time to dance;
[5]a time to cast away stones, and a time to gather stones together;
 a time to embrace, and a time to refrain from embracing;
[6]a time to seek, and a time to lose;
 a time to keep, and a time to cast away;
[7]a time to rend, and a time to sew;
 a time to keep silence, and a time to speak;
[8]a time to love, and a time to hate;
 a time for war, and a time for peace.
[9]What gain has the worker from his toil?

¹⁰I have seen the business that God has given to the sons of men to be busy with. ¹¹He has made everything beautiful in its time; also he has put eternity into man's mind, yet so that he cannot find out what God has done from the beginning to the end. ¹²I know that there is nothing better for them than to be happy and enjoy themselves as long as they live; ¹³also that it is God's gift to man that every one should eat and drink and take pleasure in all his toil. ¹⁴I know that whatever God does endures for ever; nothing can be added to it, nor anything taken from it; God has made it so, in order that men should fear before him. ¹⁵That which is, already has been; that which is to be, already has been; and God seeks what has been driven away.

There are many people for whom the Book of Ecclesiastes really means this passage, and in particular verses 1–8. Take a few moments to read it aloud. You will find yourself under its spell; the fascinating rhythm of its language, the finely balanced and contrasting experiences to which it points. It has been a passage for all seasons and all moods: from that of a young man trying to come to terms with a quickly broken marriage, to that of the girl bubbling with enthusiasm as, for her, success and love walk hand in hand; from that of a woman silently mourning the loss of a life-long companion, to that of a mother joyfully greeting the birth of her first child. "For everything there is a season, and a time . . ." (v. 1). It is all here: life—that ever-changing kaleidoscope of things which come to us unasked and outwith our control (*eg* birth and death, war and peace), as well as of moments that we can choose, like moments of silence when any words would be jarring and unhelpful, moments when we must speak since silence would only be angry and defensive. To live is to face inevitable change, and to come to terms with what can surely never be boring since it is so challengingly varied.

It is as if, when we look at life, we are gazing at a large tapestry, a tapestry finely wrought with many interweaving and contrastingly coloured threads. Every thread, every colour seems to fit into its appropriate place. We look at it and think that we ought to be able to see in it a meaningful pattern, that it must as a whole convey some meaningful message. But does it? No, says Koheleth; if there is, as no doubt there may well be, a divine purpose running through it, God has chosen not to tell us what it is, and we cannot find it out.

Let us take a closer look at verse 11, particularly the words, "he [*ie* God] has put eternity into man's mind". We can easily get the wrong end of the stick here. The Hebrew word *olam* translated "eternity" hardly means that timeless spiritual world that we so often think of as standing over and against our fleeting world of sense and time. If that were so, then Koheleth would be saying to us that when we are caught up in the busy-ness, often the rat-race of life, we need to be able to stand back from it and see everything in the light of eternity. We may not then see the whole picture— that belongs to God—but at least we can be helped to see ourselves in perspective. No doubt that is true and excellent advice. It is all too easy to rush frantically around and never stop long enough to ask where we are going or why.

That, however, is not what Koheleth is saying. The word *olam* could come from a verb meaning to conceal or to hide; in which case it would be pointing us to the 'hiddenness' in things. Coverdale translated verse 11, "He hath planted ignorance also in the hearts of men", while more recently it has been suggested that we ought to translate, "He has put in their minds an enigma". On this view Koheleth is saying to us that life sounds like a series of "Enigma Variations" to quote the title of Elgar's well known orchestral work. On the other hand, *olam* in the Old Testament usually means simply Time, time that stretches indefinitely into the past and into the future. So the New English Bible translates, "moreover he has given man a sense of time past and future, but . . .". This, I think, is where Koheleth finds himself, and he has many companions today. Life is fascinating. Not only is there a wonder in its ever-changing experiences, but we can look back across the years and the centuries, tracing the unfolding pilgrimage of the human race, and we can look forward and speculate what life may be like in the year 2000. Whether there is, however, any ultimate purpose in it, we cannot tell. God—and many today would add, if there be a God—alone knows. There is, therefore, only one thing to do: live, live life to the full as it comes to us day by day (v. 12; see comment on 2:24).

This passage ends (vv. 14–15) with Koheleth crossing swords with those who wish to claim much more. In verse 14 he recalls the words of Deuteronomy 4:2, where the people of Israel are warned that they must not tamper with the statutes and the ordinances which God has given them: "You shall not add to the word which I command you, nor take from it ..." (cf. Deut. 12:32). In Deuteronomy these words are intended to underline the need for total and unquestioning obedience to the supreme and unchanging will of God. To Koheleth, however, they merely deepen his sense of resignation. Yes, no doubt God pulls the strings always, but his purpose is inscrutable and there is nothing we can do about it. We can only bow before a mystery we cannot understand and cannot change.

It was part of the wisdom tradition in which Koheleth was nurtured that "the fear of the Lord is the beginning of knowledge" (Prov. 1:7). The fear of the Lord, however, may mean many different things. It may mean a warm, gladly-given sense of reverence, or it may point to a somewhat more chilly sense of fear or dread in the face of a God of whose intentions you cannot be sure. Koheleth is closer to this latter sense and it is tinged with a feeling of despair as he says, "God has made it so, in order that men should fear before him" (v. 14). Meanwhile we can be sure of one thing; life is not going to change (v. 15). We cannot make it different from what it has been and what it will continue to be under God's control.

The difficult concluding words of verse 15 are probably correctly paraphrased in the Good News Bible when it renders, "God makes the same things happen again and again". There is truth here. We do not control what happens to us. The same things may happen to us as have happened to other people; the crucial question is not what happens, but how we handle it. As Christians we are called to face anything that happens with a confidence and joy which were denied to Koheleth, since we know in Paul's ringing words that nothing can separate us from his love: "neither death, nor life, neither angels nor other heavenly rulers or powers, neither the present nor the future, neither the world above nor the world below—there is nothing in all creation that will ever be able to separate us from the love of God, which is ours through Christ Jesus our Lord" (Rom. 8:38–39, GNB). But to be able to say this means that the tapestry of life is no longer a puzzle, however rich, but has been woven round a human face in which we see the mystery of God's love for us.

A CRUEL ROAD WINDING TO A DEAD END

Ecclesiastes 3:16–4:3

[16]Moreover I saw under the sun that in the place of justice, even there was wickedness, and in the place of righteousness, even there was wickedness. [17]I said in my heart, God will judge the righteous and the wicked, for he has appointed a time for every matter, and for every work. [18]I said in my heart with regard to the sons of men that God is testing them to show them that they are but beasts. [19]For the fate of the sons of men and the fate of beasts is the same; as one dies, so dies the other. They all have the same breath, and man has no advantage over the beasts; for all is vanity. [20]All go to one place; all are from the dust, and all turn to dust again. [21]Who knows whether the spirit of man goes upwards and the spirit of the beast goes down to the earth? [22]So I saw that there is nothing better than that a man should enjoy his work, for that is his lot; who can bring him to see what will be after him?

[1]Again I saw all the oppressions that are practised under the sun. And behold, the tears of the oppressed, and they had no one to comfort them! On the side of their oppressors there was power, and there was no one to comfort them. [2]And I thought the dead who are already dead more fortunate than the living who are still alive; [3]but better than both is he who has not yet been, and has not seen the evil deeds that are done under the sun.

You cannot pull the wool over Koheleth's eyes. It would have been no use going to him and saying with Pippa in Browning's poem : God's in his heaven—All's right with the world! He would have said, 'Don't talk nonsense'. He knew only too well that all was not right in the world of his day, any more than it is in our world today. It would be easy to become bitter and disillusioned, as many people are today, when we look out on a world and discover that where we expect justice and fair dealing we only find injustice and corruption (v. 16). It hits us today in our personal lives when so many in our affluent Western society are caught in a poverty trap, denied opportunities for education, frustrated in their search for work, and conscious of the pain of racial discrimination. It is built into the economic system which controls the future of nations. The economy of a struggling third world country may be ruined by decisions over which it has no control—a cut in the price of oil or cocoa or coffee. Power so often lies in the hands of the oppressors, whether they recognize they are oppressors or not (4:1–2). For every one of the casualties of life who die with a Mother Teresa to comfort them, there are countless thousands who die with no-one to comfort them.

What then are we to say about human life? Koheleth begins his answer to this question in verses 17 and 18, but they are difficult to understand, with the text of verse 18 very uncertain in places. Although other interpretations are possible, I think the Good News Bible is right in putting verse 17 into quotation marks. I am well aware, says Koheleth, what people say—God will judge in his own good time—but so what? All that seems to be clear now is that God puts us through the mill to drive home to us one simple fact, that we are merely "beasts", no better than any other animal. He is not here talking about human conduct, although sometimes when we think of man's inhumanity to man and the depths to which we can sink, to call man 'The Naked Ape' seems suspiciously like an insult to the ape family. No, what Koheleth is talking about is the one thing we share with all other creatures in the world—the fact of mortality. As the New English Bible neatly translates the first half of verse 19: "Man is a creature of chance and the beasts are creatures of chance, and one mischance awaits them all: death comes to both alike". Here Koheleth is drawing on the picture of man which we find in the Creation story in Genesis 2:7: man who, like all other creatures, receives from God "the breath of life", that life-gift which one day is withdrawn; man, "formed" by God "of dust from the ground", and warned after his rebellion against God, "you are dust, and to dust you shall return" (Gen. 3:19). Whatever our abilities, whatever our achievements, we remain, in the words of the hymn: "Frail children of dust and feeble as frail".

Is there anything else to be said? Is there something within us, call it what you will, spirit or soul, which survives death and makes us different from all other animals? The New Testament does not talk about such a something, but it does offer us a Risen Lord. Koheleth can only shrug his shoulders and say 'Who knows?' There may well have been people in his own day speculating about life after death, but he has no certainty—the traditional faith of Israel had none—and where he has no certainty, he will not pretend (see comments on 2:12ff.). This life is all he knows and he calls upon us to make the most of it while it lasts (3:22). For him life is brief and cruel. Better then to be dead, for at least the dead are spared any further anguish; better still never to have been born and thus to have been spared the trouble which is our inevitable lot in life (4:2–3).

This comment is obviously very much a question of mood as well as thought. Elsewhere Koheleth is going to argue that it is better to be alive than to be dead, for at least life is real: "a living dog", he claims "is better than a dead lion" (9:4). But we are creatures of mood. There are days when we feel depressed and despondent and life hardly seems worth living; there are other days when, without anything really having changed, we face life with a quiet confidence and cheerfulness. Quite trivial things can spark off our different moods—a harsh or a helpful word, a phone call or the letter we did not receive. It is good to know that there is, here in the Bible, one who enters into our different moods, who has shared our blackest moments, who has been where we have sometimes been, and can give poignant and vivid expression to things that we sometimes find difficult to put into words or to share with other people.

WHY WORK?

Ecclesiastes 4:4–8

4Then I saw that all toil and all skill in work come from a man's envy of his neighbour. This also is vanity and a striving after wind.
5The fool folds his hands, and eats his own flesh.

⁶Better is a handful of quietness than two hands full of toil and a striving after wind.

⁷Again, I saw vanity under the sun: ⁸a person who has no one, either son or brother, yet there is no end to all his toil, and his eyes are never satisfied with riches, so that he never asks, "For whom am I toiling and depriving myself of pleasure?" This also is vanity and an unhappy business.

What makes people work? Job satisfaction ... the need to provide for themselves and their family ... the desire to be creative or to contribute something to society? No, says Koheleth, it is just "a man's envy of his neighbour" (v. 4). It is rivalry, the competitive spirit that urges you to go one better than the person next door. We want to be able to drive a more expensive and more luxurious car, send the children to a more select school, or perhaps move to a more select locality. There is something of this in all of us. It has its good side. Whatever our job or vocation we want to get to the top, or as far up the ladder as we can. We are disappointed if we don't make it. We feel cheated if someone else, with no more ability or dedication than we have, gets there before us. There is an old Jewish saying that it is the rivalry of scholars that increases wisdom. But it can all go wrong. It can lead to envy and jealousy. It can blind us to the need to come to terms with our own limitations. We shall always come across people who seem to have greater gifts than we have. How much better to rejoice in the gifts they have than to regard them with resentment. Over against this sometimes frantic desire for one-up-manship, Koheleth paints a picture of the layabout, the fool "who folds his hands, and eats his own flesh" (v. 5), ie destroys himself or, as the New English Bible puts it, "wastes away". If Koheleth sees no point in driving yourself into the ground just to go one better than other people, equally he has no time for those who will not lift a finger to help themselves or others. You have got to work, you have got to want to work. It is one of the tragedies of our increasingly technological society that there are so many people who want to work, yet have to come to terms with enforced idleness. Such idleness can be 'soul-destroying', our modern idiom for Koheleth's "eating one's own flesh".

There is the story of the young man who was only twenty-two years old and ten months married when he threw himself off a railway bridge. He left behind a bitter song of despair which began:

Up at 10, sign on the bru,
    looked in the job centre,
    nothing new;
Walked to the corner,
    seen a kid sniffing glue,
    guess there ain't nothing better to do.

Society forced this young man to "fold his hands", and he destroyed himself.

It may be that in verse 5 Koheleth is quoting a well-known proverbial saying about the idleness of a fool. In verse 6 he counters it with another proverbial saying which more nearly reflects his own attitude. Often proverbial sayings that come down to us seem to give contradictory advice; *eg* "too many cooks spoil the broth" and "many hands make light work". We can pay a heavy price for the frantic 'busy-ness' which drives us on—the stress factor that leads to physical and mental problems, the breakdown in family relationships. Equally there is a heavy price to be paid for the idleness which leads to loss of self-respect or a dropping out into the world of addiction. In verse 6, Koheleth is pointing us to the middle way, to that "handful of quietness" that is better than "two hands full of toil"; to the peace of mind that comes to those who take an honest look at themselves, accept their own strengths and limitations, and do not make impossible demands upon themselves or others. There is a moving portrait of such a person in John Berger's book *A Fortunate Man*; the country doctor in a rural backwater in England. He has no claim either to fame or notoriety, yet he works creatively, accepted as part of the community, sharing conversations and friendship, using his healing skills on body, mind and spirit, trusted, doing what he wants to do, and asking for no more. We are fortunate if we lay our hands on such "quietness".

Obviously Koheleth knows people who are not prepared to settle for such a "handful of quietness". He describes them in verses 7–8; people for whom work seems to be the be all and end all of life, lonely people who do not even have the excuse of a family to support for what they are doing. The phrase which in verse 8 describes such a person, and which the RSV translates as a person "who has no-one", is literally 'and there is no second [person]'. Who this second person is, is not clear. It could be a business partner or a wife or, as the New English Bible suggests, a friend. If such a loner would only stop for a moment to ask himself the question, 'For whom am I working and depriving myself of the good things of life?', he would soon realize that his lonely 'busy-ness' is pointless and futile. Yet it is a strange fact, isn't it, that often we seem to know the right questions to ask concerning how other people should live their lives, but remain blind to the questions we ought to be asking ourselves.

HELPFUL ADVICE

Ecclesiastes 4:9–16

> 9Two are better than one, because they have a good reward for their toil. 10For if they fall, one will lift up his fellow; but woe to him who is alone when he falls and has not another to lift him up. 11Again, if two lie together, they are warm; but how can one be warm alone? 12And though a man might prevail against one who is alone, two will withstand him. A threefold cord is not quickly broken.
> 13Better is a poor and wise youth than an old and foolish king, who will no longer take advice, 14even though he had gone from prison to the throne or in his own kingdom had been born poor. 15I saw all the living who move about under the sun, as well as that youth, who was to stand in his place; 16there was no end of all the people; he was over all of them. Yet those who come later will not rejoice in him. Surely this also is vanity and a striving after wind.

We all find ourselves in situations of having to take choices which throw light on our sense of values, on the things that are really important to us in life. Koheleth illustrates this in two areas of experience by using a common teaching technique of the wisdom writers, namely statements which say, 'A is better than B'. Thus in the Book of Proverbs we find (15:16–17):

> Better is a little with the fear of the Lord
> than great treasure and trouble with it.
> Better is a dinner of herbs where love is
> than a fatted ox and hatred with it.

(a) *Going it alone or sharing with others* (vv. 9–12).

The opening words—"two are better than one"—may be merely the statement of a general principle or they may refer to some particular relationship such as a business partnership. We must not assume that he had in mind the marriage relationship, however obvious that may be to us as an illustration of the point he is making. Indeed in the light of his cynical comments on women in 7:26–28 it is unlikely that he would apply his "two are better than one" to marriage. Go it alone, he says, and you are on your own, for better and for worse. You have no-one to pick you up, no-one to support you, when you are in difficulties. There are, of course, advantages in not being in partnership. You have only yourself to consider. But it is the disadvantages to which Koheleth is drawing our attention. If you are on your own you are more vulnerable to assault (v. 12), a situation with which we are only too sadly familiar today when people have to be warned about the dangers of walking alone, even in broad daylight, in the streets of certain parts of our large cities.

This theme is capped by what may well be a proverbial saying: "A three-fold cord is not quickly broken". There has been much speculation as to why it is a *three-fold* cord. Some have found in it a hidden reference to the doctrine of the Trinity, some believe it refers to the strengthening of the marriage bond through the coming of a child. All such speculation is unnecessary. Why is three-ply wool so popular for knitting: why do ropes which have to take a heavy strain have at least three strands in them? The interwoven three strands provide a strength far greater than one strand or even two strands can give. It is this interweaving of our lives with others which often pulls us through the sticky patches of life. To believe that we can go it alone is to court disaster.

(b) *Fame—here today and gone tomorrow* (vv. 13–16).

Although the contrast in the opening words between "the poor and wise youth" and "the old and foolish king" who is no longer teachable, is clear enough, much of the rest of this section is far from clear. Does Koheleth have a particular incident in his mind here? If so, we do not know what it is. How many characters are there in the story? Are the "poor and wise youth" and the "old and foolish king" one and the same person at different stages in life, or two different people? And who is "that youth", literally 'the second youth' in verse 15, who becomes the pin-up boy of his day? Is he to be identified with the "poor and wise youth" of verse 13 who became king, or is he another young man who in turn ousted the first young man who ousted the king? It is a real headache of a numbers game and there is no easy solution to it. But whatever the story and however many characters flit in and out of it, certain things are reasonably clear. If fame is the spur that drives men on, it can turn into an uneasy and fair-weather companion. A man may begin life in humble circumstances, willing to learn, open to the wise counsel of others. He may better himself sensationally, exchanging a prison cell for a palace. He may achieve a life-time's ambition, but at a cost, the cost of becoming a different person, arrogant, no longer willing to listen to advice. The passing years do not necessarily bring wisdom. There is no age limit to a fool! There are people who, as we say, become too big for their boots, who pay a heavy price for that power and success which can turn out to be so fickle. Today's popular hero may be tomorrow's forgotten man.

Koheleth does not play the heavy-handed moralist at this point. He just draws our attention to what happens and finds in it another illustration of the things in life which raise in his mind a large question mark as to whether there is any discernible meaning in life. We need not draw the same conclusion. Much the same scenario could lead us to ponder again the challenging words of Jesus: "What will a man gain if he wins the whole world and ruins his life?" (Matt. 16:26, JB).

DOs AND DON'Ts IN WORSHIP

Ecclesiastes 5:1–7

> [1]Guard your steps when you go to the house of God; to draw near to listen is better than to offer the sacrifice of fools; for they do not know that they are doing evil. [2]Be not rash with your mouth, nor let your heart be hasty to utter a word before God, for God is in heaven, and you upon earth; therefore let your words be few.
>
> [3]For a dream comes with much business, and a fool's voice with many words.
>
> [4]When you vow a vow to God, do not delay paying it; for he has no pleasure in fools. Pay what you vow. [5]It is better that you should not vow than that you should vow and not pay. [6]Let not your mouth lead you into sin, and do not say before the messenger that it was a mistake; why should God be angry at your voice, and destroy the work of your hands?
>
> [7]For when dreams increase, empty words grow many: but do you fear God.

Koheleth here turns his shrewd eye on what goes on in worship. He knows that people flock to the temple and do so often cheerfully and thoughtlessly. There were no doubt as many reasons for going to the temple in Koheleth's day as there are for going to church today. You may go because you enjoy the singing or are impressed by the liturgy or want to hear a certain charismatic preacher ... or for many other better or worse reasons. Here Koheleth has some relevant comments to make.

(a) "Guard your steps" (v. 1), watch it, think what you are doing. This is a warning note that we hear sounded long before Koheleth's time. A thousand years before his day, a Mesopotamian document speaks of "one who acknowledges no guilt yet rushes to his god; without thinking he raises his hands [in prayer] to his god". But only a fool would do that, says Koheleth. Think. Worship is not about enjoying yourself or participating in an aesthetically pleasing ritual; it is about 'listening' or 'obeying'. He is taking his stand in a long tradition, most noticeable in the prophets who were singularly unimpressed by temples packed with enthusiastic worshippers. Their attitude is summed up in Samuel's crushing words to Saul:

> Behold, to obey is better than sacrifice,
> and to hearken than the fat of rams.

> (1 Sam. 15:22)

Worship is not like going to a concert and coming away inspired and uplifted by great music. You can do that and remain totally insensitive to what is going on around you: indeed you can be so uplifted that common everyday things and the needs of people around you seem trivial and unimportant. But worship must never be merely spiritual self-indulgence or the satisfying of our emotional needs. It must mean listening, opening ourselves to the obedience that God wants from each one of us. It must flow out into action. As Jesus reminds us: "Not everyone who says to me 'Lord, Lord,' shall enter the kingdom of heaven, but he who does the will of my Father who is in heaven" (Matt. 7:21).

(b) Do not rush into God's presence pouring out a torrent of words, as if the more you have to say the more acceptable you will be to God: "let your words be few" (v. 2). Again we are reminded of the words of Jesus: "in praying do not heap up empty phrases as the Gentiles do; for they think they will be heard for their many words" (Matt 6:7). If Koheleth is only pleading for a little verbal economy and discipline in worship, then many of us would want to say 'amen' to that. There are times when people seem to believe that the more they say and the more passionately they say it, the more likely God is to listen. It sounds as if they had a bad connecting line to God and needed to extend the call to make sure he got the message. Words, words, words, far from bringing us nearer to God can sometimes act as obstacles between us and God.

But Koheleth has a deeper personal problem: "let your words be few" (v. 2). Why? Because "God is in heaven, and you upon earth". These are not merely words pointing us to the majesty of God and the reverence due to him. They take us close to the heart of Koheleth's religious problem. God for him is a distant remote figure. The warmth of a personal relationship with God has gone.

For all his sound advice about worship, we can hardly imagine him standing up and shouting 'hallelujah', praise the Lord. He is respectful and thoughtful, but the vital, throbbing sense of communion with God is no longer part of his experience. I doubt whether he could have said what an elderly lady once said to me. She was crippled with arthritis and for some time had been unable to go to church. Noticing a radio on a small table beside her bed, I commented that she must find it a great help to be able to tune in to the broadcast worship services. She looked at me and replied, "Laddie, I don't need the radio to take me to God. He is here whenever I need him". But for Koheleth God was not "here" on earth, he was "there" in heaven. In his experience a vital element in religion had died; but he still believed strongly in religious etiquette. Everything in worship must be done decently and in order, unmarred by any meaningless enthusiasm. There is no use criticizing him for this. This is the point he had reached in his spiritual pilgrimage. There are many people like him in our churches today.

(c) Mean what you say (vv. 4–6). Do not make promises to God and then fail to keep them. That is asking for trouble. Here, again, he is simply echoing the teaching in which he had been brought up, the teaching about 'making a vow' in the Book of Deuteronomy:

> When you make a vow to the Lord your God, you shall not be slack to pay it; for the Lord your God will surely require it of you, and it would be a sin in you. But if you refrain from vowing, it shall be no sin in you. You shall be careful to perform what has passed your lips, for you have voluntarily vowed to the Lord your God what you have promised with your mouth.

(Deut. 23:21–23)

Koheleth spells this out by insisting that it is no use taking a solemn vow in the temple, promising to give something to God in return perhaps for some experience of his goodness or in penitence for your own sins, and then later on saying "before the messenger that it was a mistake" (v. 6); I did not really mean it. Who this "messenger" is we do not know. The Hebrew word translated "messenger" can refer either to a human or a super-human figure. Most of the early translations of the Bible take it to refer to God or some angelic figure—the New English Bible's "the angel of God" follows this line. It may, however, refer to a temple messenger or official sent to collect what the worshipper has promised—thus the Good News Bible has "God's priest".

The challenge of what Koheleth is here saying must surely come home to all of us. Think back over the promises you have made, when you publicly professed your faith in church, or when you faced a particular crisis situation in your own life. Have you kept them? Don't we all fall down at this point? Don't we all try to salve our conscience by producing what we feel are good reasons for not doing certain things, but what are in effect only excuses. So often the comment our lives make on our promises is, 'I didn't really mean it'. That, says Koheleth, like the other things to which he has drawn our attention in this section, is the mark of a "fool". In verses 3 and 7 he is probably quoting proverbial sayings both of which are underlining the fact that words can be meaningless, as meaningless as dreams, particularly the words of a fool; and fools are often far from slow to express their views. Idle chatter, particularly idle pious chatter, is no substitute for a proper reverence towards God (for the meaning of the phrase "fear God" in verse 7, see comment at 3:14).

CORRUPTION

Ecclesiastes 5:8–9

> 8If you see in a province the poor oppressed and justice and right violently taken away, do not be amazed at the matter; for the high official is watched by a higher, and there are yet higher ones over them. 9But in all, a king is an advantage to a land with cultivated fields.

Corruption is a fact of life. No society has ever been totally free from it, from the Persian Imperial system of Koheleth's day to the Mafia of today. It was widespread in ancient Israel. In language very similar to that in these verses, the prophet Isaiah speaks of those in authority who misuse their power:

> to turn aside the needy from justice,
>   and to rob the poor of my people of their right

(Isa. 10:2)

In the face of this, the prophet protests vigorously and pronounces God's judgment upon it. Koheleth shrugs his shoulders and says, 'Don't be surprised: it's the system and you can't beat the system'. It is the price you pay for bureaucracy. The official you meet may be sympathetic, but he has got a higher official sitting on his shoulder. He must be consulted and satisfied. And there is a top man keeping an eye on them all. Not only does the buck get passed up the line, but in many societies, ancient and modern, at each stage someone is out to line his own pocket. The New English Bible footnote, by rendering in the final phrase of verse 8 "the Highest" with a capital 'H', reflects a tradition that sees here a reference to God. It is much more likely, however, that it refers merely to the highest official in the province or in the organization. Verse 9 is a puzzle. The one certain thing that can be said about it is said in the Good News Bible footnote, "Verse 9 in Hebrew is unclear". It may be that it is saying that against the corruption of officialdom the best hope lies in a strong central government (a king) and a thriving economy. But what if central government is itself corrupt, as many kings in Israel were, and as those holding the reins of power have been right down to the present day—witness Watergate? And even a thriving economy does not necessarily guarantee that the rights of the poor are safe-guarded. There must be a point at which we refuse to accept the system, particularly when it loads the scales heavily against those who are most at risk in society. But this is not the stuff of which Koheleth is made.

WEALTH AND CONTENTMENT

Ecclesiastes 5:10–20

10He who loves money will not be satisfied with money; nor he who loves wealth, with gain: this also is vanity.

11When goods increase, they increase who eat them; and what gain has their owner but to see them with his eyes?

12Sweet is the sleep of a labourer, whether he eats little or much; but the surfeit of the rich will not let him sleep.

13There is a grievous evil which I have seen under the sun: riches were kept by their owner to his hurt, 14and those riches were lost in a bad venture; and he is father of a son, but he has nothing in his hand.

¹⁵As he came from his mother's womb he shall go again, naked as he came, and shall take nothing for his toil, which he may carry away in his hand. ¹⁶This also is a grievous evil: just as he came, so shall he go; and what gain has he that he toiled for the wind, ¹⁷and spent all his days in darkness and grief, in much vexation and sickness and resentment?

¹⁸Behold, what I have seen to be good and to be fitting is to eat and drink and find enjoyment in all the toil with which one toils under the sun the few days of his life which God has given him, for this is his lot. ¹⁹Every man also to whom God has given wealth and possessions and power to enjoy them, and to accept his lot and find enjoyment in his toil—this is the gift of God. ²⁰For he will not much remember the days of his life because God keeps him occupied with joy in his heart.

There are few of us who are not fascinated, perhaps even fewer who are not a little envious when we see a snooker star or a golfer receiving a winner's cheque for £45 000, or hear of a TV star signing a soap opera contract that guarantees her a million dollars. Money is part of our lives. We need it for ourselves and those dependent upon us. If we are below the poverty line, life can be a misery. There is nothing wrong with money, but Koheleth posts some warning signs that we need to heed.

(a) There is the love of money (v. 10); that craving for money and all it stands for, which can become addictive. It is a craving that can never be satisfied, since the more we get the more we want. It can turn a man into a compulsive gambler. It fuels the ambitions of a ruthless business tycoon. At a humbler level we buy a black and white TV set, then we need and must get a colour TV, then we need and must get a video, then ... And so it goes on, an endless craving which, as Koheleth says, is really pointless; it does not make sense, it is *hebel*, "vanity". It is not only pointless; it can become central to our lives. As 1 Timothy 6:10 puts it: "For the love of money is a source of all kinds of evil. Some have been so eager to have it that they have wandered away from the faith and have broken their hearts with many sorrows" (GNB).

(b) Wealth attracts hanger-ons (v. 11). The more you have, the more people there are only too willing to sponge off you. You suddenly find that you have a lot of good-time friends, only too anxious to help you to spend what you have. Such a swarm of hanger-ons, warns Koheleth, can prevent a man from enjoying what he has: and what is the point of having it, if you cannot enjoy it? The verb translated "to see" means, as often in Ecclesiastes, "to enjoy"; and "to see them with his eyes" means to enjoy for himself.

(c) Wealth can lead to over-indulgence (v. 12). The "surfeit of the rich" should probably be taken to mean over-eating. Such over-indulgence undermines health and leads to sleepless nights, a sad contrast to the workman with modest means who enjoys a good night's sleep. It is one of the ironies of life today in our affluent Western society that having eliminated many of the crippling diseases associated with poverty, our killer diseases are now the diseases of affluence: coronary attacks, lung cancer, liver failure. We over-indulge and then spend millions on diet control and low calorie foods. We purchase our exercise machines to tone up the body we have been neglecting and undermining.

But if wealth has its danger notices which must be posted, there is also a larger question mark which must be placed beside it. Koheleth draws our attention to this by citing in verses 13–20, a case history with which he is familiar. It is the story of a man who, with single-minded ruthlessness, devoted all his energies to acquiring wealth. Then came the crash. One "bad venture" (v. 14), perhaps an unfortunate investment or an unlucky business deal, and it was all gone, leaving both him and his family destitute. A life-time of toil and sweat and the end result is nothing. As his life comes to an end he possesses no more than when he entered it, naked "from his mother's womb". This says Koheleth, twice over, is a "grievous evil" (vv. 13, 16) or a sickening tragedy; the kind of thing that really knocks you out. It all seems so pointless.

How then should we come to terms with life? Here he takes us back to the advice he has already given in 2:24 (see comment there). Life is short (v. 18); but that is no reason for being miserable. Accept life as it comes to you as "a gift of God" (v. 19). Live it to the full day by day. If it so happens that you are blessed with wealth and possessions, thank God for that and use them to bring joy into your life. The more joy you can pack into your life, the less likely you are to be depressed by the fact life is short and the years swiftly passing.

It is hard to accept that this is all that there is to be said about life; but it is equally hard not to admire the courage and the very positive attitude to life that Koheleth has. He may not have the answer to some of the questions that haunt us, but he throws down the gauntlet to us to live life to the full. He would regard it as a sin against God not to do so. There are Christians who sometimes give the impression that the answers they have mean that they ought to run away from life or feel guilty about enjoying it. Koheleth however would rather, I believe, have approved of the view so well-expressed by Dietrich Bonhoeffer:

"I am sure that we ought to love God in our *lives* and in the blessings he sends us. We should trust him in our lives, so that when our time comes we may go to him in love and trust and joy. But, speaking frankly, to long for the transcendent when you are in your wife's arms is, to put it mildly, a lack of taste, and it is certainly not what God expects from us. We ought to find God and love him in the blessings he sends. If he pleases to send us some overwhelming earthly bliss, we ought not to try to be more religious than God himself."

(*Letters and Papers from Prison,* p. 86)

IT'S AN UNJUST WORLD

Ecclesiastes 6:1–12

[1]There is an evil which I have seen under the sun, and it lies heavy upon men: [2]a man to whom God gives wealth, possessions, and honour, so that he lacks nothing of all that he desires, yet God does not give him power to enjoy them, but a stranger enjoys them; this is vanity; it is a sore affliction. [3]If a man begets a hundred children, and lives many years, so that the days of his years are many, but he does not enjoy life's good things, and also has no burial, I say that an untimely birth is better off than he. [4]For it comes into vanity and goes into darkness, and in darkness its name is covered; [5]moreover it has not seen the sun or known anything; yet it finds rest rather than he. [6]Even though he should live a thousand years twice told, yet enjoy no good—do not all go to the one place?

[7]All the toil of man is for his mouth, yet his appetite is not satisfied.

⁸For what advantage has the wise man over the fool? And what does the poor man have who knows how to conduct himself before the living? ⁹Better is the sight of the eyes than the wandering of desire; this also is vanity and a striving after wind.

¹⁰Whatever has come to be has already been named, and it is known what man is, and that he is not able to dispute with one stronger than he. ¹¹The more words, the more vanity, and what is man the better? ¹²For who knows what is good for man while he lives the few days of his vain life, which he passes like a shadow? For who can tell man what will be after him under the sun?

"There's aye something," as the saying goes. People whom we may envy, people who seem to have everything that we would desire to make the good life possible, don't always enjoy it. Koheleth provides us with two illustrations of this:

(a) Here is a well-to-do, highly respected man, who can have all the things he desires, yet "God does not give him power to enjoy them" (v. 2). It may be that crippling ill health or death strikes suddenly. Someone else—"a stranger"—then reaps the benefit of all that he has. Surely, says Koheleth, that is pointless and "all wrong," to give the Good News Bible's rendering of "it is a sore affliction".

(b) Here is another man (v. 3) who is the living embodiment of what the truly good life—*shalom*—meant in Old Testament times; a man with a large family, a man who lives to a ripe old age. Yet he gets no real satisfaction out of life and dies unlamented, without even a decent burial. The phrase translated "and also has no burial," *ie* he dies unlamented, may also be rendered "even if he has a proper burial". This then would be another plus in his life story—a long fruitful life capped by an appropriate funeral. But even that, says Koheleth, could not compensate for the fact that he got no satisfaction out of life. It would have been better if he had been still-born. At least he would have been spared the hassle of life. It is not length of life that matters; however long you live, in the end you go the way of all flesh. It is the *quality* of life that is important, and life is meaningless unless it brings joy, satisfaction and happiness.

From these illustrations of what is "all wrong" in life, Koheleth turns in verses 7–9 to look at another side to the wrongness in life.

To do so he makes use of two proverbial sayings—one in verse 7, the other in verse 9—which seem to contradict each other. It is as if he began with 'the grass is always greener' and ends with 'a bird in the hand is worth two in a bush'. The saying in verse 7 draws our attention to the fact that people are on a treadmill from which they can never escape, a treadmill which leaves them forever dissatisfied. The more they get and earn, the more they want (see comments on 5:10ff.). If that is in general true, is a wise man any better off than a fool? He leaves us with the question, but we already know that his answer to that can only be 'yes' and 'no': 'yes' in as much as the wise man does have clues about how life ought to be lived, clues that are denied to the fool; 'no' in so far as death comes to both alike, and not even some of the wisest of men know the answer to life's ultimate questions. Then as if to balance all the snags he has previously pointed out to us in the possession of wealth, Koheleth raises a question about "the poor man" in verse 8. Suppose, he says, there is a poor man who knows how to cope with daily living—so what? There are obviously so many of the good things in life which a poor man, in Koheleth's eyes, can never have, just because he is poor. Deprivation is deprivation, whatever shape or form it takes. No romanticizing here about the value of the poor and simple life! It is as if Koheleth is casting his eye over all sorts and conditions of men—rich and poor, the wise and the fools—and saying to us that not one of them has found the key to unlock the innermost secrets of life. Whatever their status in society, whatever their IQ, whatever their bank book may say, they are all caught in a maze and no-one knows how to solve its puzzle. You are forever dissatisfied? Best not to expect too much and you will not be disappointed. Don't waste your time longing for what you can never have. This seems to be the point of the saying in verse 9.

If all this seems fairly defeatist, it is based on Koheleth's conviction, expressed in verses 10–12, that it is not in our power to decide what life is all about. It comes to us with its hallmark already upon it, and there is no use trying to argue about it. You may wish it were different, but wishing will not alter the facts. If anyone tries to argue about it he finds himself arguing with "one stronger than he" (v. 10), *ie* God, and that is like battering your head against a brick wall. Life is short. There are no certain and absolute values in it. We don't even know what lies round the next corner.

There is an interesting contrast here between Koheleth and certain other Old Testament thinkers who share many of his perplexities. Life does not make sense, says Koheleth, it does not make sense . . . it does not make sense. Life does not make sense, says Job, it does not make sense . . . but it *must* make sense. So Job insists on struggling, searching, arguing with God in the belief that he is arguing not only with "one [who is] stronger than he", but with one who is also just. Koheleth gives up and advises us to settle for what we have got. It may not be much, but it is all we are going to get.

Even people with a much more robust faith sometimes find themselves in situations where they come very close to Koheleth, and are forced to say 'it does not make sense'. Listen to C. S. Lewis in the immediate aftermath of the tragic death of the woman he had loved so deeply and so briefly (*Shadowlands*, p. 10):

> "Where is God? Go to him when your need is desperate, when all other help is vain, and what do you find? A door slammed in your face, and a sound of bolting and double bolting on the inside. After that, silence. You might as well turn away. The longer you await the more emphatic the silence will become. There are no lights in the windows. It might be an empty house. Was it ever inhabited? It seemed so once . . ."

Yet C. S. Lewis did not turn away. He waited, he agonized, he struggled—you can relive his pilgrimage in *A Grief Observed*—he struggled until he discovered the truth of what he put onto the lips of one of the characters in another of his books: "I know now, Lord, why you utter no answer. You yourself are the answer. Before your face questions die away. What other answer would suffice? Only words, words, words, to be led out to do battle against other words . . ." (quoted from *Shadowlands*, p. 152). The trouble with Koheleth is that for him God himself cannot be the answer. God is an enigma, a distant enigma in heaven, while he has to come to terms with so much that he cannot understand here on earth.

HOME TRUTHS

Ecclesiastes 7:1–9

¹A good name is better than precious ointment;
  and the day of death, than the day of birth.
²It is better to go to the house of mourning
  than to go to the house of feasting;
 for this is the end of all men,
  and the living will lay it to heart.
³Sorrow is better than laughter,
  for by sadness of countenance the heart is made glad.
⁴The heart of the wise is in the house of mourning;
  but the heart of fools is in the house of mirth.
⁵It is better for a man to hear the rebuke of the wise
  than to hear the song of fools.
⁶For as the crackling of thorns under a pot,
  so is the laughter of the fools;
  this also is vanity.
⁷Surely oppression makes the wise man foolish,
  and a bribe corrupts the mind.
⁸Better is the end of a thing than its beginning;
  and the patient in spirit is better than the proud in spirit.
⁹Be not quick to anger,
  for anger lodges in the bosom of fools.

This section is built round six brief sayings, probably proverbs, each in one of the typical wisdom forms,—'A is better than B' (see comment on 4:9ff.). The sayings have been carefully chosen to illustrate certain things that are close to the heart of Koheleth's thinking. Sometimes he adds to them his own wry comments. The sayings are often much sharper than can be conveyed in any English translation. The RSV translation of the first one—"A good name is better than precious ointment"—uses eight English words; the original Hebrew uses only four. The English translation moreover hides the fact that "good" and "precious" are different translations of the same Hebrew word, and that there is in the Hebrew a play on the similarity of sound in the words translated "name" and "ointment". Try saying the Hebrew: *tov shem mishemen tov*.

Let us look briefly at the six sayings in turn.

The *first* saying, "A good name is better than precious ointment" (v. 1) reminds us that there are certain things, important things, that we either have or do not have, and that if we do not have them nothing can take their place. They are things that money cannot buy. Which would you rather be, a person with a name or reputation for honesty and integrity, who can hold his head high and look other people straight in the face, or someone who has everything that money can buy, yet is regarded by other people as unscrupulous and untrustworthy? There may, however, be another undertone to this saying. At birth a child is given a name, a name that may very well indicate the happiness that the child has brought or the hopes for the future of the child. So Abraham and Sarah called their long hoped for child Isaac, 'he laughs' (see Gen. 21:3–6); in the same way we might give a girl the name Felicity. Precious ointment, on the other hand, is associated with death. Remember the story in Mark 14:3ff., where at Bethany in the house of Simon the leper, a woman pours a jar of precious ointment over Jesus' head. He brushes aside the criticism of her impulsive extravagance with the words, "She has anointed my body beforehand for burying" (Mark 14:8). The day of birth, with its associated naming of the child, is a happier occasion than the day of death with its anointing ointment. It may well be that Koheleth is turning this saying upside down with his wry comment that it is the day of death that is better than the day of birth (see 4:2–3)

This thought leads into the *second* and *third* sayings in verses 2 and 3, where Koheleth again homes in on the one fact in life we can never side step or shrug off—the fact of our mortality. He reminds us that there are things we learn when face to face with sorrow, "in the house of mourning", which we do not and cannot learn in the midst of happiness, "in the house of feasting". Think of our typical family gatherings. We gather to celebrate the birth of a child or a baptism, or a twenty-first birthday or a marriage. On such occasions our thoughts are naturally of joy, of the rich possibilities in human life, of our hopes for the future—and rightly so. But we meet again at a family funeral. Our thoughts are then very different; we are reminded of the fragility of human life, of the end to which we all come. But what is meant in the words "by sadness of countenance the heart is made glad" (v. 3)? It may be that the Good News Bible is right in taking "heart" to mean "mind" and in translating it as sorrow "may sadden your face, but it sharpens your understanding"; it teaches you things you might otherwise not learn. Yet there is the curious fact to which many people have borne witness out of their own experience; that in the midst of sorrow there can be found a deep sense of joy that nothing can destroy. Koheleth may well have met it in the lives of people he knew. It is a joy which can be immeasurably strengthened when we can say with Paul that our earthly bodies are no more than a temporary tent, one day to be taken down as we journey on to "a house God himself has made, which will last for ever" (2 Cor. 5:1, GNB). Koheleth has no such hope, but he knows that to live life at a superficial laughter level is the mark of a fool in contrast to the outlook of a wise man.

This leads him to the *fourth* saying which features "the wise" and "fools" (v. 5). It is not always comfortable to be in the presence of the wise. They are liable to tell you some home truths that may hurt. Fools, on the other hand, will not upset you. They are far more likely to sing your praises. The Book of Proverbs makes much the same point in terms of the contrast between a friend and an enemy (27:6):

> Faithful are the wounds of a friend;
> profuse are the kisses of an enemy.

The mask is torn off fools in verse 6 through a very effective play on the similarity in sound of the words translated "thorns" and "pot"; and indeed the same sound echoes in the word for "song" in verse 5. The laughter of fools is dismissed as being like the "crackling of thorns" as the firewood burns up under a pot; it is noisy, self destructive. We make something of the same point in our saying 'empty barrels make most noise'. Of course *we* are not fools like that, are we? We naturally think of ourselves as being among those who have their heads screwed on the right way, who know a thing or two about life, *ie* "the wise" in Koheleth's way of thinking. As if to sound a warning, Koheleth points out that even the wise have their weak spots. No-one is exempt from temptation. Even the wise may succumb, misuse the power they have, or become susceptible to bribery (v. 7). It is always easy to look at other people who have gone wrong and say, 'I would never have done that; I'm not that kind of person'. Yet we all have our breaking points and we never know what we might or might not do in certain circumstances. There is an old Jewish saying, "Do not trust in yourself until death". That is why we pray, and need to pray, as Jesus taught us:

> ". . . do not bring us to the test,
> but save us from the evil one."

> (Matt. 6:13, NEB)

Sayings *five* and *six* come in verse 8 and are linked in theme. We all know people who can quickly become fired with enthusiasm for something, whether it is getting a new pet, learning a musical instrument, or working for Christian Aid. But the enthusiasm wanes. It is not as easy as they thought; there are snags or something else comes along to catch their fancy. So they give up; they never see things through to a successful, worthwhile conclusion. That, says Koheleth—and maybe there is something of that in most of us—is no good: "Better is the end of a thing than its beginning". There are other people who work away happily at something; then somebody criticizes them and they stalk off in high dudgeon. Their pride has been offended: 'if that's what so and so thinks, let him do it himself'. That also, says Koheleth, is no good. Be patient, stick at it. To be easily upset, to harbour anger or resentment is the mark of a fool. As Proverbs puts it (14:17, GNB):

> People with a hot temper do foolish things;
> wiser people remain calm.

It is in line with this that in the Letter of James, the nearest thing in the New Testament to a wisdom book, we are told to be, "quick to listen, slow to speak, and slow to anger. For a man's anger cannot promote God's right purposes" (James 1:19–20, NEB). Next time you are tempted to give up something in disgust, or to fly off the deep end, remember Koheleth's words (v. 8, GNB):

> The end of anything is better than its beginning.
>   Patience is better than pride.

BE SENSIBLE

Ecclesiastes 7:10–14

> [10]Say not, "Why were the former days better than these?"
>   For it is not from wisdom that you ask this.
> [11]Wisdom is good with an inheritance,
>   an advantage to those who see the sun.
> [12]For the protection of wisdom is like
>   the protection of money;
> and the advantage of knowledge is that
>   wisdom preserves the life of him who has it.
> [13]Consider the work of God;
>   who can make straight what he has made crooked?
> [14]In the day of prosperity be joyful, and in the day of adversity consider; God has made the one as well as the other, so that man may not find out anything that will be after him.

Like many other wisdom teachers, Koheleth has his feet planted firmly on the ground. He does not invite you to dream dreams or build spiritual castles in the air. Look elsewhere if that is what you want. He invites you to be sensible about life.

(a) *Be sensible about the past.* There are people—there always have been people—who moan about the terrible state the world or society or the Church are in; people who longingly want to go back to what they call 'the good old days'. Then, so we are told, churches were full every Sunday, children never spoke back to their parents, right was right, wrong was wrong, and everyone knew the difference between the two. Koheleth's comment is 'stuff and nonsense'. As the Good News Bible translates verse 10: "Never ask, 'Oh, why were things so much better in the old days?' It's not an intelligent question". It is not an intelligent question because the good old days were in many respects the bad old days. Many people who wish they had been living a hundred years ago amid the solid values of Victorian society would come quickly running back to today, with all its problems, if their wish were granted. If I had been living a hundred years ago, I would have been in danger of being tried for heresy for writing a book like this. For most people in the city of Glasgow a hundred years ago, life was far more grim than it is today, with all the problems of deprivation that we face. To romanticize about the good old days, however, is as useful a way as any of running away from the challenge and the opportunities of the present.

(b) *Be sensible about your own life here and now*. To enjoy life, says Koheleth, you need two things—wisdom and money (vv. 11–12). For him both wisdom and money are a necessary part of the insurance policy he wants to take out against the risks of life. Not for him the call of holy poverty, nor the belief that you will find the secret of life by renouncing all earthly possessions. He wants the security that wisdom can bring, the wisdom that helps you to see where you are going in life (see 2:13ff.). He wants the security that material possessions bring; and he does not see any contradiction between these two things. Neither do most of us see any contradiction in the way we live day by day; nor should we. It is the essence of Christian stewardship for most of us that we have a certain income, we enjoy material possessions, and we must learn to use them responsibly under God. There is no justification for altering the text here in order to say, as the New English Bible does, that "wisdom is better than possessions . . . Better have wisdom behind you than money". That may be what certain high sounding moralists and preachers would have wanted him to say. But that is not what he says. He is working on a much more down-to-earth sensible level.

(c) Life, as he says to us in verses 13–14, is as God has made it, and there is no use wishing it were otherwise. You have got to be prepared to take the rough with the smooth, "the day of adversity" as well as "the day of prosperity", and come to terms with them both. You can never know what is going to happen next. He is very close to saying what we find well expressed in the words of William Freeman Lloyd's hymn:

> My times are in thy hand,
> Whatever they may be;
> Pleasing or painful, dark or bright,
> As best may seem to thee.

Yet the chill remoteness of his God would have prevented him from saying with the next verse:

> My times are in thy hand,
> Why should I doubt or fear?
> My Father's hand will never cause
> His child a needless tear.

He believes in providence, but it is a rather sterner providence than we meet with in some other parts of the Old Testament (see Ps. 139; Isa. 49:14–15); and it is not yet a providence whose inner meaning is laid bare in "Jesus the Crucified".

DON'T TEMPT PROVIDENCE

Ecclesiastes 7:15–22

[15]In my vain life I have seen everything; there is a righteous man who perishes in his righteousness, and there is a wicked man who prolongs his life in his evil-doing. [16]Be not righteous overmuch, and do not make yourself overwise; why should you destroy yourself? [17]Be not wicked overmuch, neither be a fool; why should you die before your time? [18]It is good that you should take hold of this, and from that withhold not your hand; for he who fears God shall come forth from them all.

[19]Wisdom gives strength to the wise man more than ten rulers that are in a city.

[20]Surely there is not a righteous man on earth who does good and never sins.

²¹Do not give heed to all the things that men say, lest you hear your servant cursing you; ²²your heart knows that many times you have yourself cursed others.

We begin with a problem which has haunted the thoughts of men of faith in all ages. If this is God's world, why is it that good and godly people so often seem to get a raw deal, while evil and godless people flourish? It is a question we find being asked in some of the Psalms (eg Psalm 73); it is a question that Job asks and continues to ask, demanding an answer, in spite of his friends' pious insistence that it is not a serious question. To Koheleth it is not a question; it is just a fact (v. 15), a fact from which he draws what has been regarded as a cynical conclusion—do not be either too good and too wise or too wicked and too foolish. Since neither being "righteous" nor being "wicked" guarantees anything, do not go overboard in either direction. The normal, sensible life will be a mixture of both; and religion will square the books for you.

Is this, as one commentator has suggested, 'the shabby and self-regarding side of common sense'? Perhaps . . . perhaps it is no more than the outlook of the average decent man who is not going to murder his wife, even if he occasionally fiddles his tax returns; a man who is not going to sacrifice himself or his own comfort for others in need, even if he does go to church fairly regularly. It is neither the stuff of martyrs nor of criminals. But not many of us are called to be either. In the striking and challenging way, however, in which he puts his case, may Koheleth not be warning us of something that we all too easily forget, that it is often the 'unco guid' and the spiritual know-alls, the overwise of verse 16, who are just as great a menace to themselves and others as the most decadent and unscrupulous rogues? There are few villains in the events that lead up to the Cross; there are many good men, the sincere spiritual leaders of the Jewish people, so sure that they were right, that Jesus could only be seen as a threat to the God-given ideals for which they stood. Why not give Koheleth credit for seeing the potential menace in the 'over-righteous' as well as in the 'over-wicked'? Given that life faced him with an insoluble moral puzzle, it is not surprising that he comes out saying, 'Take it easy!'.

It is not that Koheleth doubts the value of wisdom. He never does. Wisdom, he claims, is of more value to a wise man "than ten rulers that are in a city" (v. 19). It may be that he has in mind here "the council of ten" who were normally responsible for civic affairs in the Hellenistic cities of his day. If so, it is hard to say whether he is being somewhat cynical about the local politicians—a favourite pastime of those who do not want to get their own hands dirty—or whether he is commending their usefulness but asserting that wisdom has a greater claim to be of value. We must not let our own views about politicians colour our judgment at this point! Wisdom is of value . . . yes, but don't look for perfection. You will not find it. There is no-one who ever gets it right all the time, says Koheleth: everyone makes mistakes. We should not read into verse 20 any deep theological meaning. Koheleth is merely warning us not to go around demanding or expecting perfection. If we do, we are liable to be disillusioned. Nor must you listen, he says, to everything you hear, or you are liable to get hurt. Who among us, after all, could honestly claim that we have never said anything hurtful about other people (v. 21)?

In all this we are hearing the words of a man who has had to come to terms with a world he does not understand, and who therefore does not see the point in making too great claims either for himself or for others.

THE FUTILE SEARCH

Ecclesiastes 7:23–29

23 All this I have tested by wisdom; I said, "I will be wise"; but it was far from me. 24 That which is, is far off, and deep, very deep; who can find it out? 25 I turned my mind to know and to search out and to seek wisdom and the sum of things, and to know the wickedness of folly and the foolishness which is madness. 26 And I found more bitter than death the woman whose heart is snares and nets, and whose hands are fetters; he who pleases God escapes her, but the sinner is taken by her. 27 Behold, this is what I found, says the Preacher, adding one thing to another to find the sum, 28 which my mind has sought repeatedly, but I

have not found. One man among a thousand I found, but a woman among all these I have not found. 29Behold, this alone I found, that God made man upright, but they have sought out many devices.

In chapter 1, verse 13, Koheleth tells us that he had embarked on a voyage of exploration to discover the meaning of all that goes on in life. He had journeyed to strange lands and had come up with some unexpected conclusions. He now gives us his considered verdict on the voyage. The object of his journey, that treasure of wisdom which could provide the key to unlock the secret of what life is all about, has proved elusive. He has searched, he has failed to find. It remains forever beyond his grasp, deep, "deeper than man can fathom" (v. 24, NEB). We are reminded of the magnificent hymn to Wisdom in Job 28 (vv. 12–14). It speaks of man's achievements, but then asks:

"But where shall wisdom be found?
    And where is the place of understanding?
Man does not know the way to it,
    and it is not found in the land of the living.
The deep says, 'It is not in me,'
    and the sea says, 'It is not with me.'
It cannot be gotten for gold,
    and silver cannot be weighed as its price."

'Amen' to that says Koheleth, but does he take the next step with Job 28:23 and say with quiet conviction: "God understands the way to it, and he knows its place"?

In Job 28:28, God speaks to man and says, "Behold, the fear of the Lord, that is wisdom; and to depart from evil is understanding". The present Book of Ecclesiastes ends on a very similar note, inviting us to a life of simple faith and goodness: "Fear God and keep his commandments" (12:13). Yet there is so much else in the book which suggests that Koheleth's was a far more troubled mind which did not have such a faith (see comments on 12:12–14). Certainly he does not express such a faith here. He can only say that at the end of the voyage he has returned home empty-handed.

The riddle of the universe remaining dark and unsolved, he turns the spotlight (vv. 25 ff.) onto the deviousness and stupidity which characterize human nature and human relationships. He comes up with a very harsh and jaundiced view. There is a strong streak of oriental male chauvinism running through the Old Testament. We hear much, particularly in the Wisdom literature, of men's views on women, but little of women's views on men (the exception, as we shall see, is in the Song of Solomon). Many of the views on women are highly uncomplimentary:

Better to live alone in the desert
    than with a nagging and contentious wife!
(Prov. 21:19, NEB)

Endless dripping on a rainy day—
    that is what a nagging wife is like.
(Prov. 27:15, NEB)

Yet this is balanced in, for example, Proverbs 31:10ff. and Ecclesiasticus 26:13ff. by a sympathetic picture of the good capable wife, pre-women's lib model of course.

Like the sun rising in the heights of the Lord,
    so is the beauty of a good wife in her well ordered home.
(Ecclesiasticus 26:16)

Koheleth's view is uncompromisingly uncomplimentary. His experience with women, he claims, is "more bitter than death" (v. 26). You are a lucky man if you escape from her clutches. Not one woman has he found to come up to his expectations. What lies behind such bitter comments? Was he tied to a nagging wife? Had he been involved in some unfortunate sexual entanglements which had soured his view of the opposite sex? We do not know. It looks as if he would have agreed in spirit with the comment of one of the early Church Fathers who said that Satan, having stripped Job of all that was precious to him in life, left him his wife because Satan thought that she would greatly assist him in conquering this saint of God! If he had a jaundiced view of women, he is not much less jaundiced in his view of men. Not a single woman had come up to his expectations, and "only one man among a thousand" (v. 28). Statistically it is not very impressive. We can only wonder what company he kept. How much of this was his own fault? Was he too coldly and intellectually cynical ever to enter into lasting and meaningful human relationships? You can spend so much time trying to dissect life that you forget how to live it.

On one thing, however, Koheleth is clear. If people turn you off and human nature is perplexingly devious, it is no use blaming God. Drawing on the creation stories that we find in Genesis chapters 1–3, he insists that God "made man upright", and if it has all gone wrong, it is man's own fault, "they have sought out many devices" (v. 29) or, as the Good News Bible has it, "we have made ourselves very complicated". It was common enough in the ancient world to blame the gods for the evil which was rampant in the human race, just as today people will blame 'the stars' or 'satanic forces' or 'the system', anything other than themselves. Koheleth will have none of this. Look no further than yourself, he says; look to what is so graphically portrayed in the Garden of Eden story in Genesis chapters 2–3, to that misuse of the freedom that God has given us.

YES MINISTER

Ecclesiastes 8:1–9

¹Who is like the wise man?
  And who knows the interpretation of a thing?
 A man's wisdom makes his face shine,
  and the hardness of his countenance is changed.
²Keep the king's command, and because of your sacred oath be not dismayed; ³go from his presence, do not delay when the matter is unpleasant, for he does whatever he pleases. ⁴For the word of the king is supreme, and who may say to him, "What are you doing?" ⁵He who obeys a command will meet no harm, and the mind of a wise man will know the time and way. ⁶For every matter has its time and way, although man's trouble lies heavy upon him. ⁷For he does not know what is to be, for who can tell him how it will be? ⁸No man has power to retain the spirit, or authority over the day of death; there is no discharge from war, nor will wickedness deliver those who are given to it.

⁹All this I observed while applying my mind to all that is done under the sun, while man lords it over man to his hurt.

The purpose of the wise men in many societies in the ancient Near East was to draw attention to the attitudes and actions which led to a successful life. Nowhere was it more important to know this, to be aware of correct etiquette, than in what we would call the upper ranks of the Civil Service. There is an Egyptian document from some two thousand years earlier than Koheleth, *The Instructions of the Vizier Ptah-hotep*, which is in effect the Civil Servant's handbook, a manual on how to be a successful official of the state. It gives advice, among other things, on how the budding courtier should behave when dining out with a superior. No picking at the food placed before you, no rude stares. It goes on: "Let your face be cast down until he addresses you. Speak only when he addresses you. Laugh after he laughs, and it will be pleasing to his heart, and what you do will be pleasing to his heart. No-one can know what is in the heart".

Koheleth here presents us with his own brief manual on how to succeed at court. He begins with a general statement about the "wise man" and the skills and graces which will stand him in good stead. He must know "the interpretation of a thing" (v. 1), that is to say, he has got to know the way the wind is blowing. He must be pleasant, courteous, with no hint of stubbornness or obduracy in his make-up. The key to success is obedience—"because of your sacred oath", literally "an oath of God". Verse 2 should probably end as in the Hebrew text with the words "your sacred oath", but most English versions add to this verse the next two words in Hebrew translating as in the RSV "be not dismayed", or as in the Good News Bible and the New English Bible "do not be precipitate", which take the words to refer to an act which is rash or hurried. But what does this "sacred oath" or "an oath of God" mean? It has been taken to mean that the oath of loyalty you give to human authority is limited by the higher loyalty you have sworn to God. There are many illustrations of this in Scripture; from Daniel's three friends—Shadrach, Meshach and

Abednego—defying the edict of the king of Babylon (Dan.ch.3), through Daniel himself disobeying Darius' proclamation (Dan.ch.6), to the words of Peter and John, before the Jerusalem council: "You yourselves must judge which is right in God's sight—to obey you or to obey God" (Acts 4:19, GNB). There has always been a point at which Christians throughout the ages have invoked a higher loyalty than loyalty to the state. It is a live issue today for many Christians as they find themselves increasingly driven to civil disobedience in face of the nuclear threat.

It is more likely, however, that the "sacred oath" of which Koheleth speaks, refers to the solemn oath of obedience given to the authority of the powers that be; an oath of obedience to which you must remain faithful, claims Koheleth, even when "the matter is unpleasant" (v. 3); *ie* even when you are ordered to do something which is personally distasteful. Never give the impression of being anxious to leave the king's presence, and never delay to implement a policy even if it does not meet with your approval. The king's authority is unchallengeable. You are not there to question it, only to obey. It is still the Civil Service remember. Asked if he did not consider a recent government policy unfair, a senior civil servant replied: "as a humble civil servant I cannot comment on the system". The attitude of the wise civil servant is, 'Yes minister'. He will seek to avoid trouble. If he is wise he will know when and how to act and to speak (v. 5). It is at this point that the attitude of court officials, including prophets who belonged to the political establishment, differed sharply from that prophetic voice of protest which did not hesitate to say a word displeasing to those in authority. For a classic illustration of this see the story in 1 Kings chapter 22 of the clash between Micaiah ben Imlah and the 400 court prophets.

The thought of knowing how and when to act or speak—the "time and way" (v. 5)— leads Koheleth in verses 6ff. to look at this 'how' and 'when' in a wider context, the context of life as a whole. It is as if he casts his mind back to chapter 3 and remembers, yes, there is a time and a place for everything. The snag is that, at this point, man finds himself in a real spot of trouble and perplexity. He has no assurance about what the future will bring, except for one thing: the certainty of death (see 2:14). And as the Good News Bible neatly translates the second half of verse 8, "That is a battle we cannot escape; we cannot cheat our way out". In the first half of verse 8 the word translated by the RSV as "spirit", Hebrew *ruah*, can mean either spirit/life or wind. So it may be taken as a reference to man's inability to control the wind, symbol of his powerlessness in the face of death (NEB); or it may refer simply to man's powerlessness to hold on to life no matter how desperately he may wish to do so. This double meaning of the word is effectively used by Jesus in his conversation with Nicodemus: "The wind blows where it wills, and you hear the sound of it, but you do not know whence it comes, or whither it goes. So it is with every one who is born from Spirit" (John 3:8, see further the comments on 11:4). The final word does not lie with us and no amount of diplomatic skill can alter that fact. Meanwhile, in this world in which there are so many things that we cannot arrange, we must come to terms with those in authority over us, an authority which can often be repressive and hurtful (v. 9).

We would be unwise to try to draw from this section any general guidelines as to what our attitude should be towards 'the powers that be'. Koheleth is not presenting us with any theory of the state nor any thoughts for or against civil disobedience. He has a more limited purpose; to give advice on how to succeed in government service. That means coming to terms with the fact that you are a person under authority; there to implement decisions not to question them. Thus we are reminded that in a much broader sense we are all under authority. There are circumstances outwith our control which we cannot question: we cannot avoid death.

BAFFLED

Ecclesiastes 8:10–17

[10]Then I saw the wicked buried; they used to go in and out of the holy place, and were praised in the city where they had done such things. This also is vanity. [11]Because sentence against an evil deed is not executed speedily, the heart of the sons of men is fully set to do evil.

¹²Though a sinner does evil a hundred times and prolongs his life, yet I know that it will be well with those who fear God, because they fear before him; ¹³but it will not be well with the wicked, neither will he prolong his days like a shadow, because he does not fear before God.

¹⁴There is a vanity which takes place on earth, that there are righteous men to whom it happens according to the deeds of the wicked, and there are wicked men to whom it happens according to the deeds of the righteous. I said that this also is vanity. ¹⁵And I commend enjoyment, for man has no good thing under the sun but to eat, and drink, and enjoy himself, for this will go with him in his toil through the days of life which God gives him under the sun.

¹⁶When I applied my mind to know wisdom, and to see the business that is done on earth, how neither day nor night one's eyes see sleep; ¹⁷then I saw all the work of God, that man cannot find out the work that is done under the sun. However much man may toil in seeking, he will not find it out; even though a wise man claims to know, he cannot find it out.

There are many things that baffle Koheleth, not least the fact that, whatever we may think ought to be the case in God's world, it is the wicked who often flourish and the good who go to the wall. If this baffles Koheleth, the opening verse (v. 10) in this section is, and always has been, baffling to scholars. Beyond all the detailed difficulties in the text—and there are several—there are two broad lines of interpretation.

(a) The whole verse refers to "the wicked". They are described as frequenting the temple during their lifetime or as being given a good send off at the end of the day with crowds of mourners flocking to the cemetery. The words translated "the holy place" could refer either to the temple or to the burial ground. Whichever it may be, these "wicked men" are loudly praised in the very city in which they pursued their devious ends. Maybe it is just a case of *de mortuis nil nisi bonum,* as the Latin tag goes, even if there was not much good that could be said about them in their lifetime. Maybe it is because such people often gain popularity during their lifetime because in certain respects they can be successful. This, after all, is one of the standard arguments in favour of a dictator: Mussolini made the trains run on time, Hitler took Germany out of economic chaos.

(b) The verse contains within it a contrast, with the second half being translated, 'those who acted uprightly are forgotten in the city'; a sad contrast to the popularity of the wicked.

Is Koheleth upset by this picture of the pseudo-pious wicked and their popularity, or does he simply note it as one of those facts of life which are there whether we like it or not? We do not know. He does, however, go on to ask the question as to why it is that people do turn to crime to further their own ends. His answer is that they get away with it; crime pays because they are not swiftly punished. The greatest deterrent to crime, he is arguing, must be the certainty of being caught. But it does not happen that way. The chances of being caught and punished are not high. The forces of law and order seem to have had much the same problem in his day as in ours.

The Good News Bible is, I believe, right in putting the second half of verse 12 and the whole of verse 13 in quotation marks and introducing them with the comment: "Oh yes, I know what they say: 'If you obey God, everything will be all right, but it will not go well for the wicked . . . they will die young, because they do not obey God'". Here Koheleth is taking issue with the widely held view that the wicked perish and come to an early sticky end, while people who obey God, prosper and live to a ripe old age. Don't believe it, he says; that is nonsense. Life does not work out like that. Often what happens to good people is what you might expect to happen to evil people, and vice versa. We don't go far in life before we are brought face to face with that kind of situation and find ourselves asking, 'Why did it have to happen to her of all people?' To Koheleth this is senseless and baffling. He takes refuge in his oft repeated advice: there is only one thing to do, get on with the business of living, while life lasts (v. 15, see comment on 2:24).

He is far too much of a realist, however, not to admit that there are other people who obviously do not share his views. There are those who "claim to know" (v. 17); claim to know far more than he does, claim to know the basic principles on which the world works and the purposes of God that shape it. Koheleth's only comment on this is to say: 'Don't believe them; they may claim to know, but they don't know. You can keep a round the clock watch on all that goes on so feverishly in this world, and you would still be no nearer discovering what it all adds up to'. He has a point. Philosophers and thinkers, including Koheleth, have come and gone. Often they have been sharply critical of the shortcomings of their predecessors. Each has had a contribution to make to human understanding; some at a deeper level than others. All may be drawing our attention to certain things that are important for our understanding of life: but are we any nearer solving the riddle of this baffling world? Perhaps human thought alone will never be able to take us to this point. We may have to be humble enough to accept that the answer lies in God's gift of himself to us. But that means believing that, "The Word became flesh and dwelt among us" (John 1:14) and that, "God was in Christ reconciling the world to himself" (2 Cor. 5:19). It means accepting what the world dismisses as folly, the folly of the Gospel, and discovering that the foolishness of God is wiser than men (see 1 Cor. 1:18–25).

PROVIDENCE?

Ecclesiastes 9:1–10

¹But all this I laid to heart, examining it all, how the righteous and the wise and their deeds are in the hand of God; whether it is love or hate man does not know. Everything before them is vanity, ²since one fate comes to all, to the righteous and the wicked, to the good and the evil, to the clean and the unclean, to him who sacrifices and him who does not sacrifice. As is the good man, so is the sinner; and he who swears is as he who shuns an oath. ³This is an evil in all that is done under the sun, that one fate comes to all; also the hearts of men are full of evil, and madness is in their hearts while they live, and after that they go to the dead. ⁴But he who is joined with all the living has hope, for a living dog is better than a dead lion. ⁵For the living know that they will die, but the dead know nothing, and they have no more reward; but the memory of them is lost. ⁶Their love and their hate and their envy have already perished, and they have no more for ever any share in all that is done under the sun.

⁷Go, eat your bread with enjoyment, and drink your wine with a merry heart; for God has already approved what you do.

⁸Let your garments be always white; let not oil be lacking on your head.

⁹Enjoy life with the wife whom you love, all the days of your vain life which he has given you under the sun, because that is your portion in life and in your toil at which you toil under the sun. ¹⁰Whatever your hand finds to do, do it with your might; for there is no work or thought or knowledge or wisdom in Sheol, to which you are going.

Koheleth never doubts that the world we live in is God's world. Like Hamlet he believes, "There's a divinity that shapes our ends,/Rough hew them how we will". We are all "in the hand of God" (v. 1). That he believes, but that is not enough. Are we merely play-things in God's hands? What kind of God is this? What is the nature of that divinity or providence that shapes our ends? Koheleth can only conclude: we do not know. Is it "love or hate"? Some English translations try to wriggle out of this uncomfortable conclusion to verse 1. The Jerusalem Bible renders, "Man does not know what love is or hatred": while the Good News Bible makes the love and hate refer to the passions of the righteous and the wise, and transfers the words 'Man does not know' to the beginning of a second sentence: "No-one knows anything about what lies ahead of him". But Koheleth's words should not be twisted in this way, just because we do not like what he says. He puts it quite bluntly: there is a God who controls our lives as he rules the universe, but whether his purposes are friendly or hostile, "whether it is love or hate", we do not know. We need not be surprised at this verdict. It is in line with his oft repeated view that everything is *hebel,* that life just does not add up. It is hard to see how he could say anything else, since there are so many things in life that puzzle and perplex him.

The rest of chapter 9 sets out to remind us of some of these puzzling things. We begin with our old friend, Death, who has been hovering in the wings and sometimes stepping forward to occupy centre stage ever since 2:14. Death is no respecter of persons, Koheleth reminds us. We may not like it, we may even try to avoid thinking about it. It is what he calls "an evil" (v. 3), but it comes to good folk and to bad folk alike; to those who are punctilious in their religious observances and to those who are not; to those who go to church and to those who never darken the door of a church. We will go down to "the dead"; we have all been issued with a one way ticket to *Sheol* (v. 10).

Sheol is for the Hebrews the shadowy underworld which is the abode of the dead. Many other words are used in the Old Testament to describe it. Most of them draw a bleak, chill picture. It is the "Pit" (Ps.16:10); it is Abaddon or "Destruction" (Prov. 15:11), a place of darkness and oblivion. The Book of Job graphically describes it as:

> ... the land of gloom,
> a land of deep darkness ...
> a land of gathering shadows, of deepening darkness,
> lit by no ray of light, dark upon dark.
>
> (Job 10:21–22, NEB)

It is not hell in the sense of a place to which some people go—the wicked—to be punished. Sheol means for everyone the end of all that makes life meaningful and joyful. It was widely believed that in Sheol no contact with God was possible. The author of the Book of Ecclesiasticus gives voice to a view which we find elsewhere in the Old Testament:

> Who in the netherworld can glorify the Most High?
> ....
> No more can the dead give praise than those who have never lived:
> they glorify God who are alive and well.
>
> (Ecclesiasticus 17:27–28, cf. Isa. 38:18–19)

Sheol is a grey and featureless landscape with all that is real and worthwhile totally absent.

It is for this reason that Koheleth quotes with approval the proverbial saying: "a living dog is better than a dead lion". At least where there is life there is hope (v. 4). There is always something to look forward to, always a possible tomorrow. To live is to know, to know something, even if it is only that you are going to die. To be dead is to know nothing. It is the end of all that life has to offer; its experiences and its passions. There is no sense here of someone tired of the hassle of life, longing for 'restful death'. Quite the opposite: it is life and life alone that is real. Better to face the perplexities and questions of life than to step into the nothingness of death. On his death bed, Thomas Hobbes said: "I am about to take my last voyage, a leap into the dark". For Koheleth that "dark" was chill and unattractive. The only certainty he knew was the light of life.

It is not surprising, therefore, that he comes back to and develops his, by this time well-known, theme. Enjoy life, make the most of it; not because it is a regrettable second best, but because doing so bears the stamp of God's approval (v. 7). Pull out all the stops. "Let your garments be always white" (v. 8). White is the colour of joy and celebration. Think forward to the picture in Revelation 7:9ff. of the great gathering of peoples from all nations, standing before the throne, "clothed in white robes, with palm branches in their hands", celebrating the salvation that has come to them from God. Think of a white wedding. White, and as a further sign of happiness let there be oil on your head. As Proverb 27:9 puts it: 'Perfume and fragrant oils make you feel happier'. Although Koheleth's views on women, as expressed in 7:26ff., are somewhat jaundiced, nevertheless he can hardly deny that they are there and that they can be a source of happiness. "Enjoy life with the wife whom you love" or perhaps with a woman you love, NEB, v. 9). We know nothing about Koheleth's views on marital fidelity. Although most of our English versions do not reflect this, *twice* in the Hebrew of verse 9 there occurs a phrase which the RSV translates "all the days of your vain life", literally 'all the days of your *hebel*'. It acts like a haunting refrain, underscoring his belief that there are no answers. There is, however, no use sitting down and moaning that life does not make sense. It is there to be enjoyed ... as long (v. 10) as it lasts.

LIFE'S A LOTTERY

Ecclesiastes 9:11–18

[11]Again I saw that under the sun the race is not to the swift, nor the battle to the strong, nor bread to the wise, nor riches to the intelligent, nor favour to the men of skill; but time and chance happen to them all.

¹²For man does not know his time. Like fish which are taken in an evil net, and like birds which are caught in a snare, so the sons of men are snared at an evil time, when it suddenly falls upon them.

¹³I have also seen this example of wisdom under the sun, and it seemed great to me. ¹⁴There was a little city with few men in it; and a great king came against it and besieged it, building great siegeworks against it. ¹⁵But there was found in it a poor wise man, and he by his wisdom delivered the city. Yet no one remembered that poor man. ¹⁶But I say that wisdom is better than might, though the poor man's wisdom is despised, and his words are not heeded.

¹⁷The words of the wise heard in quiet are better than the shouting of a ruler among fools. ¹⁸Wisdom is better than weapons of war, but one sinner destroys much good.

It is not only the thought of death that raises questions in Koheleth's mind about providence; it is equally what happens during our life. There seems to be no rational pattern in it. What happens to people does not seem to bear any relationship to their abilities or their skills. It may be some comfort to us if we are poor and unappreciated to be told that "intelligent men do not always get rich, and capable men do not always rise to high positions" (v. 11, GNB); but why should life be like that? It seems as if it is just a lottery. That is not the only problem. At any moment something may happen to us over which we have no control, something totally unexpected. We are at the mercy of "time and chance". Bad luck can ruin our prospects. One moment like fish swimming freely in the sea, the next caught in a net; one moment like a bird soaring in the sky, the next trapped, struggling helplessly in a snare (v. 12). That's life, says Koheleth.

He then further emphasizes this in verse 13ff. *either* by recalling an incident (well-known perhaps to himself and his first readers, but totally obscure to us, in spite of a great deal of scholarly detective work) *or* by telling us a brief illustrative story or parable. It is the story of a small town besieged by a vastly superior enemy force. In the town lived "a poor wise man". What this poor wise man did, or might have done, depends on how we interpret the second half of verse 15:

(a) The RSV translation assumes that this poor wise man through his wisdom, perhaps through some shrewd advice which he gave, delivered the town from its enemies. His reward?—'No-one remembered him'. The story is thus a classic illustration of ingratitude. You may do things to help other people but do not expect to be thanked or rewarded for doing them. You are just as likely to be forgotten, especially if you are a person of little importance or standing in the community. How often indeed do we all forget even to say 'thank you' for the services other people render to us?

(b) Other English translations (*eg* GNB, NEB) assume that this poor wise man *could* have saved the town through his wisdom; the only snag was that no-one thought of asking him. Because he was poor, a man of little or no importance in the eyes of the civil and military authorities, no-one paid any attention to him. The story is then an illustration of that snobbery or prejudice which makes us listen, or not listen, to people not because of what they have to say, but because of who they are. It is the snobbery which makes it difficult for us to swallow our pride and accept advice, often good advice, from those we regard as our social or intellectual inferiors. In such situations our natural reaction is to say, 'Who does he think he is?' We do it all the time, refusing to listen to what is being said because of our views of the person who is saying it. A party political broadcast comes on TV. Switch it off, is the response, it is only socialist propaganda or conservative clap-trap. We hear Mr Gorbachev or President Reagan putting forward proposals on the nuclear missile issue, and our immediate response is to think this is Russian or American propaganda. We do it within the Church. Don't listen to him, he is not 'sound' theologically, or he is a dyed-in-the-wool fundamentalist. So we don't listen . . . and it is to our impoverishment. He *could* have saved the town: but who was he after all? Only a poor wise man, so no-one listened to him.

This section ends with two brief comments: the *first* one in verse 17 stresses the value of wisdom; the *second* in verse 18 points to its limitations. Do not judge things, says Koheleth, by their decibel output. The quiet, calming word of a wise man may be much more effective than orders shouted at fools. The "shouting of a ruler" in verse 17 may well be that of a military commander barking out orders at the far from intelligent troops under his control. The thought, therefore, naturally moves to that of wisdom being "better than weapons of war". If that were obvious to Koheleth, how much more obvious ought it to be to us today? This, the wisdom that is better than weapons of war, we must learn, or cease to exist on planet earth. But what assurance is there in human affairs, especially in politics, that such wisdom will prevail? There is none. All the good intentions in the world, all the wise words spoken, may founder on "one mistake" (NEB, a better translation than "one sinner" in v. 18). One mistake, often a trivial mistake, can have disastrous consequences: 'for want of a nail the shoe was lost; for want of a shoe the horse was lost; for want of a horse the rider was lost; for want of a rider the kingdom was lost ... and all for want of a nail'. One mistake—this is the razor's edge on which we all live today; one error of judgment, one accidental pressing of a button, and the writing is on the wall for civilization as we know it.

SOUND ADVICE

Ecclesiastes 10:1–4

> ¹Dead flies make the perfumer's ointment give off an evil odour;
>   so a little folly outweighs wisdom and honour.
> ²A wise man's heart inclines him toward the right,
>   but a fool's heart toward the left.
> ³Even when the fool walks on the road, he lacks sense,
>   and he says to every one that he is a fool.
> ⁴If the anger of the ruler rises against you, do not leave your place,
>   for deference will make amends for great offences.

From 10:1 to 11:6 we find Koheleth in his role of a typical wisdom teacher. It is a section in the book which might well have appeared in the Book of Proverbs. It ranges over a wide variety of topics and makes us stop and think, as it offers shrewd advice, based on keen observation of human nature and the way in which society functions. Although there is no one theme running through the whole section, our attention is repeatedly drawn to the contrast between 'the wise' and 'the fool', and even when they are not mentioned, it is the attitudes of these contrasting characters which are put under the microscope in a variety of personal and social situations.

We begin in verse 1 with a thought that is close to that on which the previous section ended: it does not take much to destroy something of beauty and value. The illustration he uses is that of a perfumer using all his know-how to produce an expensive, fragrant ointment. All his skill however is in vain if, unnoticed to him, there are mixed in with the ointment, dead or dying flies. The end result will then be a putrid rather than a seductive smell. To change the picture we might think of buying a second hand car. In the showroom it looks in perfect condition; on the road it runs smoothly. But, unknown to us and not apparent on inspection, there is a small patch of rust. It begins to spread and soon we are faced with major expenditure. Just a tiny patch of rust, yet deadly and costly. So it is with "a little folly", says Koheleth; it "outweighs wisdom and honour", or as the New English Bible, with a slight alteration of the text, reads, it makes 'wisdom lose its worth'. "A little folly"—the small things that we often think do not matter, the half truth or that 'harmless' lie that gets us out of trouble for the moment, the fiddle in filling up the tax return, the letter we know should have been written and was not. But such small things can be insidious things, working away to undermine our moral fibre, leading ultimately to serious consequences for ourselves and our relationships with other people.

Verses 2 and 3 turn to the contrast between the wise man and the fool. Although I have heard it thus quoted, admittedly with tongue in cheek, verse 2 is not there to give you advice on how to vote at the next election! In many languages the right hand becomes the symbol of skill or success, no doubt because the right hand is the one most naturally used by most people. Even God always uses his right hand:

> Thy right hand, O Lord, glorious in power,
>   thy right hand, O Lord, shatters the enemy.

(Exod. 15:6)

In the great parable of judgment in Matthew 25:31ff., the sheep, acceptable to God, are placed on his right, while the rejected goats are placed on the left. Our English word 'dexterity', meaning skill or cleverness, comes from the Latin word for the right hand; whereas sinister, meaning harmful or threatening, comes from the Latin word for the left hand. If we are suspicious of something someone has said to us or about us, we refer to a 'left-handed' compliment. All of this is no doubt a gross slander on naturally left-handed people, but that is how language has developed.

It may be that the Good News Bible is correct in translating verse 2, "It is natural for a wise man to do the right thing, and for a fool to do the wrong thing", but equally it might mean that the attitude of a wise man leads to success, while that of a fool leads to failure or trouble. The difference between a wise man and a fool, says Koheleth, is clear for all to see. A fool has only got to take a stroll along the road to show his true colours. His stupidity will be apparent to everyone he meets. This is a theme that the Book of Proverbs touches on in several different ways, for example:

In everything a prudent man acts with knowledge,
but a fool flaunts his folly.

(Prov. 13:16)

There is a saying, 'there's none so blind as they that will not see'. It is the price you pay for being a fool, says Koheleth, that you do not or cannot see your own folly, the folly you so clearly reveal to other people.

The New English Bible's translation of the concluding words of verse 3 is also possible; "he calls everyone else a fool". This points us to another side to human folly. We are often tempted to think of other people, particularly those with whom we disagree violently, as plain stupid. This is one of the most effective ways of ensuring that we do not do what is far more difficult, *ie* take an honest look at ourselves and our views. That would open up the dangerous possibility that we might be wrong.

In verse 4 we are in the world of 'Yes Minister' (see comment on 8:1–9). There is no use handing in your resignation whenever the boss tears a strip off you for making a mistake. There is only one sensible response to such a situation, and that is to show "deference", to take it calmly, to pour oil on troubled waters. The same word which the RSV here renders as "deference" is used in Proverbs 15:4, in a phrase which the New English Bible translates as "a soothing word". You must be prepared says Koheleth, to accept criticism, not least when it is justified. This is something many of us find difficult to do. In the face of criticism we are far more likely to go on to the defensive, often a rather beligerent defensive. Tempers rise. Calm it, is Koheleth's advice.

THINK BEFORE YOU ACT

Ecclesiastes 10:5–11

> 5There is an evil which I have seen under the sun, as it were an error proceeding from the ruler: 6folly is set in many high places, and the rich sit in a low place. 7I have seen slaves on horses, and princes walking on foot like slaves.
> 8He who digs a pit will fall into it;
>   and a serpent will bite him who breaks through a wall.
> 9He who quarries stones is hurt by them;
>   and he who splits logs is endangered by them.
> 10If the iron is blunt, and one does not whet the edge,
>   he must put forth more strength;
>   but wisdom helps one to succeed.
> 11If the serpent bites before it is charmed,
>   there is no advantage in a charmer.

You often learn a lot about people by finding out what upsets them. In verses 5–7 Koheleth describes a situation which he finds upsetting; "an evil" he calls it. It is a situation which clearly reveals his essentially conservative, upper-class cast of mind. This evil he attributes to "an error proceeding from the ruler". The word translated "ruler" here is a different Hebrew word from that translated "ruler" in verse 4, and probably indicates a much greater sense of authority. Early commentators found in the word a reference to God the Ruler or even to His Majesty the Devil. It is far more probable that the ruler is an earthly ruler, someone who holds the reins of power in the community. Whoever this ruler was, he committed an error of judgment: he allowed what Koheleth considers the natural social order to be undermined. Influential posts in the community are held by fools, while the "rich" have no real power or influence.

Notice the assumption that it is the rich, probably the landed aristocracy, who ought to hold positions of power and prominence in public life. It is the rich not the wise, who are in the opposite camp from folly in verse 6. This is possibly a natural assumption for Koheleth to make, since in his day only the rich would have either the influence or the leisure to acquire the skills needed for government. One imagines that Koheleth would be at home in the Monday Club in Britain today, or would be on the right wing of the Republican party in the USA. The social order of which he approves assumes that everyone has and knows his rightful place in society. Yet, much to his horror, he has seen slaves, who ought to be on foot, riding on horses, and "princes", men of high rank, having to walk. It is as if he had seen someone driving up to the Social Security office in a Rolls Royce to collect his welfare benefits, while someone who naturally moved among the social élite could not afford the fare for a taxi to take him home. We may allow him his political prejudices. We cannot imagine him taking to the streets in support of the revolution. His prejudices were the natural prejudices of the circles in which he moved. Many of our political, and religious, prejudices are similarly influenced by the circles in which we move.

Koheleth's attitude, however, might lead us to stop and think as to how we are to use the Bible to help us to make political judgments. There are within the Bible powerful voices of protest, demands for justice and fair sharing, a challenging 'bias towards the poor'. Yet there is very little in the way of direct criticism of the social structures of the day. Even Jesus seems to have taken them for granted. He tells the story of the way a man deals with his servant who comes in after a hard day's work on the estate:

"Do you tell him," Jesus asks, "to hurry and eat his meal? Of course not! Instead you say to him, 'Get my supper ready, then put on your apron and wait on me while I eat and drink; after that you may have your meal'" (Luke 17:7–8, GNB). Jesus tells that story with a purpose, to underline the need for the disciple's total obedience. But there is no hint in it of any criticism of the social life he is describing. Paul similarly accepts by and large the social institutions of his day, including slavery and male domination. The Bible can no more be used merely as a hand-book for revolution than it can be paraded as uncritical support for the status quo.

Koheleth may be too uncritical of the status quo, but he is well aware that if you change things you do not necessarily change them for the better. This warning is sounded in two neat pictures in verse 8: dig a pit and watch out, you yourself may fall into it; pull down a wall, and you may find yourself bitten by a snake which has been lurking on the other side. Although these may be general warnings about the desirability of thinking carefully about the possible consequences of doing something before you do it, they may also have a political bite to them. Many a revolutionary has helped to destroy a detested, unjust social system, only to die at the hands of a revolutionary tribunal he helped to create. Western democracies may be dismissed as decadent and lacking in social conscience, but if the present leaders of Russia and China are to be believed, the so-called people's democracies have their own serious social problems. Change the system—and it may need to be changed—but don't think that by doing so you bring in the kingdom of God.

Two further illustrations in verse 9 challenge us to face realistically the dangers involved in certain things that we do. A workman in a quarry may be injured by the stones he is dislodging; a forester may be endangered by the tree he fells. Put in other more familiar terms; if you play with fire you are in danger of being burnt. More often than not, however, we do not recognize that we are playing with fire until it is too late—that harmless flirtation, the somewhat questionable things we have done over and over again which do not seem to have got us into any trouble. But the forester may have felled hundreds of trees before the one that crushed him. And the things that we do and say have a nasty habit of catching up with us sooner or later.

Although there are minor difficulties in the text of verse 10, we are all familiar with the situation it depicts. Use the wrong tool or an inefficient tool and the job in hand takes twice as long and very often demands the expenditure of much unnecessary energy. The skilled craftsman makes sure that the axe he uses is sharp *before* he begins his work. It is easy to see when it is put like that, but perhaps not so easy to recognize in our lives. Don't we often go rushing into things, barging ahead, justifying ourselves that we are busy, that we are doing something, without first stopping to think whether this is really the right way to handle this situation or to deal with that person? The need for forethought before getting involved is then beautifully and with a touch of dry humour brought home to us in verse 11. With deadly swiftness a snake strikes: not much point then in the victim complaining or protesting, 'But I'm a snake charmer!' Such pictures, illustrations that stick in the mind—these are the marks of a good teacher.

THE FOLLY OF BEING A FOOL

Ecclesiastes 10:12–15

> [12]The words of a wise man's mouth win him favour,
>   but the lips of a fool consume him
> [13]The beginning of the words of his mouth is foolishness,
>   and the end of his talk is wicked madness.
> [14]A fool multiplies words,
>   though no man knows what is to be,
>   and who can tell him what will be after him?
> [15]The toil of a fool wearies him,
>   so that he does not know the way to the city.

Don't be a fool: that, in a nutshell is the message of this section. It begins with a brief look at the contrast between the words of a "wise man" and the speech of "a fool", but thereafter it concentrates entirely on the fool. A wise man's words are described as being characterized by 'grace', Hebrew *hen*. Most of our English translations assume that this means that they "win him favour" or honour. It is more likely that the reference is to the inherent graciousness or kindliness in the words of such a man. He is not out to criticize. He is not continually tearing strips off other people to humiliate them or to undermine their self-confidence. He does not go in for destructive ridicule. The words of a fool, on the other hand, do destroy; they "consume" him just as surely as they are hurtful to other people. The outcome of his talk is "wicked madness", or, as the New English Bible translates, "mischief run mad". He uses words to stir up trouble: the nagging criticism, the snide comments, the innuendos—we have all suffered from them. Our immediate response to Koheleth's words of course is to say, 'Yes I know who he means, but we are not to be classified among the fools, are we?' Perhaps not, but the letter of James in chapter 3 gives urgent warnings to all Christians about the dangers of the tongue, the tongue which is "like a fire. It is a world of wrong, occupying its place in our bodies, and spreading evil through our whole being . . . It is evil and uncontrollable, full of deadly poison. We use it to give thanks to our Lord and Father, and also to curse our fellow man who is created in the likeness of God" (James 3:6, 8–9, GNB). Have we never used words to destroy?

Koheleth draws our attention to another mark of the fool. A fool, he says, "multiplies words" (v. 14). He does not know when to keep quiet. He goes on and on spouting nonsense (cf. Prov. 15:2) quite oblivious to the fact that it is nonsense. The trouble is that he believes what he says. The more he talks, the more he convinces himself that he knows. He has got all the answers. He has eliminated the unknown from his vocabulary. Any sense of bowing humbly before the mystery of life has gone. It takes a wise man to know when to say, 'I don't know'.

The fool not only kids himself that he is a Mr Know-All, but he usually makes life needlessly difficult for himself by being stupid over quite simple things. The last line of verse 15, 'he does not know the way to the city', is probably a proverbial saying describing a person who can be guaranteed to get things wrong. He is the kind of person who, if you took him along the street and turned him round two or three times, would not be able to find his way home; the kind of person to whom you give clear directions, but who ends up on the other side of town. The last thing a fool can do is to recognize his own limitations.

POWER AND RESPONSIBILITY

Ecclesiastes 10:16–20

> ¹⁶Woe to you, O land, when your king is a child,
>   and your princes feast in the morning!
> ¹⁷Happy are you, O land, when your king is the son of free men,
>   and your princes feast at the proper time,
>   for strength, and not for drunkenness!
> ¹⁸Through sloth the roof sinks in,
>   and through indolence the house leaks.
> ¹⁹Bread is made for laughter,
>   and wine gladdens life,
>   and money answers everything.
> ²⁰Even in your thought, do not curse the king,
>   nor in your bedchamber curse the rich;
> for a bird of the air will carry your voice,
>   or some winged creature tell the matter.

We begin by taking a look at the ingredients in a responsible, stable society. Anarchy, says Koheleth, is no substitute for firm social order. A stable society is only possible provided there is effective and wise leadership from the top (vv. 16–17). A country is unfortunate, therefore, if it has as its ruler "a child". The Hebrew word *na-ar,* translated "child", can cover a wide age range from babyhood up to the age of marriage. Jeremiah applies this word to himself when he tries to wriggle out of answering God's call to him to be a prophet. It probably indicates his sense of youthful inexperience (Jer.1:6). The word can also mean a servant or slave, just as "boy" used to be used in this sense in colonial rule. So the New English Bible translates, "when a slave has become its king", a situation which would be the total reversal of the natural social order in Koheleth's eyes (see comment on

10:5–7). This provides a neat contrast to that effective government which comes from "the son of free men" or the nobility (v. 17). On the whole, however, it seems best to stick with the RSV or its Good News Bible equivalent: "A country is in trouble when its king is a youth". It is too much to expect effective leadership from one who is young and inexperienced, especially when he is surrounded by decadent courtiers and advisers, whose major interest lies in their own personal pleasure. They "feast in the morning" (v. 16), *ie* they spend all night carousing and are still going strong in the morning; a sure-fire recipe for a monstrous hangover. A country is fortunate, on the other hand, if its ruler comes from the ranks of the "free men", the landed aristocracy, and if he is supported by responsible advisers, who do not spend all night over their cups and who are noted for their self-control, not for their drunkenness (v. 17).

Centuries before Koheleth, the prophet Isaiah had some bitter words to say about the corrupt leadership in Israel in his day: "Heroes of the wine bottle! Brave and fearless when it comes to mixing drinks! But just for a bribe you let guilty men go free and you prevent the innocent from getting justice" (Isa. 5:22, GNB). We may not agree with Koheleth's assumption that political leadership ought to come from the upper classes, but we can at least share his concern about the quality of such leadership and his abhorrence of that decadence in high places which can ruin a nation. The twentieth century is only too sadly familiar with corrupt regimes, basking in the outward symbols and wealth, creaming off personal fortunes into international banks, while their people live in crippling squalor and in fear. We have the right to expect much from our political leaders; the right to expect that the government will be responsibly run for the welfare of the whole community, rather than for party considerations or for personal prestige and fortune.

It looks as if in verse 18 Koheleth turns for a moment from the responsibilities of politicians to those of a house owner. As many a house owner has found out to his cost, if you neglect a leaking roof you can soon be in serious trouble. As the proverb "a stitch in time saves nine" reminds us, it never pays to be negligent. It may be, however, that Koheleth still has the politicians in mind, and is using this illustration to drive home to them his theme; that disaster befalls a country when its leaders neglect to live up to their responsibilities.

Not that Koheleth would ever want to don the mantle of a kill-joy! There is nothing wrong, he says, in the pleasure derived from a good meal and the wine that goes with it. But what does the last part of verse 19 mean? The RSV translates, "and money answers anything", whatever that means. The NEB renders, "and money is behind it all"; the good life is only possible provided you have the hard cash to sustain it. This would fit in with Koheleth's general outlook. Money is one of God's good gifts. Use it properly and it brings the good life within your grasp. It is also possible to translate, "but money is the concern of all": even the rich cannot be entirely carefree in their pleasures; they have still got to balance the books. Needless and thoughtless extravagance is not the mark of responsible leadership.

Nor is undercover plotting. We have two sayings that come close to aspects of the delightful picture he draws in verse 20. When we hear something and do not wish to disclose our source of information we say, "A little bird told me"; perhaps closer still are the words "even walls have ears". Don't harbour revolutionary thoughts, says Koheleth, even in the privacy of your own bedroom. It is a dangerous game. Again he is laying his cards on the table. Anything remotely resembling a theology of revolution or liberation theology was just not part of his make-up. He belonged to the ruling class; he believed in firm government. He pleads for such power and privilege to be used responsibly, but he has no sympathy for anyone who wishes to undermine the powers that be. We would be unwise to sit in judgment upon him without knowing a great deal more than we do about the society in which he lived. We would be better wrestling with the question as to how power is to be used responsibly in the society and in the world in which we live today.

NOTHING VENTURE NOTHING WIN

Ecclesiastes 11:1–6

[1]Cast your bread upon the waters,
　　for you will find it after many days.
[2]Give a portion to seven, or even to eight,
　　for you know not what evil may happen on earth.
[3]If the clouds are full of rain,
　　they empty themselves on the earth;
　and if a tree falls to the south or to the north,
　　in the place where the tree falls, there it will lie.
[4]He who observes the wind will not sow;
　　and he who regards the clouds will not reap.
　[5]As you do not know how the spirit comes to the bones in the womb
of a woman with child, so you do not know the work of God who makes
everything.
　[6]In the morning sow your seed, and at evening withhold not your
hand; for you do not know which will prosper, this or that, or whether
both alike will be good.

The opening verse in this section is a famous and much quoted
verse, particularly in the form in which it appears in the RSV and
in earlier English translations. It has usually been taken as an
invitation to be charitable or generous even when such generosity
seems to offer no forseeable harvest. Be generous, however: you
can never tell, perhaps "after many days", sometime in the future
you will reap a reward. But this is not an invitation to be generous
so that you may reap a reward. That would be against the spirit of
true generosity. That would be like counting the slices and weighing up whether you ought to give a slice away, rather than casting
your bread upon the waters. You do not look for a reward when
you are generous, but often, and sometimes in unexpected ways,
a reward comes. It is generous people, people who spend their
lives giving of themselves to others, who find that, when they are
in need, they have a host of friends. It is selfish people, who close
their hearts to others, who end up finding that they may have
plenty of this world's goods but no real friends. Read Dickens'
Christmas Carol with its transformation of Mr Scrooge from a
"squeezing, wrenching, grasping, scraping, clutching, covetous

old sinner" into a man whose "heart laughed". It came about when he was willing to cast his bread upon the waters, and "give a portion to seven, or even to eight"; that is to say, to many people.

Most other modern translations, however, suggest a rather different approach to this verse. Thus the New English Bible: "Send your grain across the seas, and in time you will get a return. Divide your merchandise among seven ventures, eight maybe, since you do not know what disasters may occur on earth" (cf. GNB). If you are in business or in trade, you must be prepared to take risks. Export or perish! If you are wise, however, you will spread the risks: you will not put all your eggs in one basket. You never know when or where bad luck may strike. It may be that in verse 1 we are dealing with a proverbial saying which is close to our 'nothing venture nothing win'. It will apply to the world of business, but it may also have a much wider relevance to our lives.

Verses 3 and 4 remind us that there are some things in life that lie totally outside our control. We can do nothing about them. Heavy clouds darken the sky. It is going to rain, even if we have been hoping and praying for fine weather for that beach picnic. A giant tree begins to topple over. It is no use telling it to fall in the opposite direction because that is where you would prefer it to lie. Where it is going to hit the ground has already been decided. We are wise if we come to terms with the fact that there are things in life over which we have and can have no control, instead of spending our time wishing that life were otherwise or saying if only things were different. In response to a certain lady who was reported as having said, "I accept the universe", Thomas Carlyle replied, "Gad, she'd better!" We don't choose the country or the family into which we are born. We don't decide the age to which we shall live—not unless we commit suicide. We can't change the colour of our skin or our IQ. We can't stop the clock or prevent the years from swiftly passing. Such things are not ours to choose.

But there are other things which we can and must do. There are decisions which are ours to take day by day. Too often we look for excuses to put off until tomorrow what we know we ought to do today, and more often than not we find them. Thus we are like the farmer, says Koheleth, who looks out and decides that the wind is not in the right direction for sowing that field, or who sees a cloud in the sky and decides that the weather is not settled enough for him to bring in the harvest. So we put off and put off, until sometimes it is too late. We put off, waiting for an ideal time to come, confident that we will recognize it when it does come. Perhaps it will never come. Remember, says Koheleth, there is so much that we do not know and cannot know. Here he plays on the different meanings of that Hebrew word *ruah,* correctly translated "wind" in verse 4 (see comment on 8:8).

It may be that the meaning of wind continues into verse 5 in which case you can follow the reading in the RSV footnote: "As you do not know the way of the wind, or how the bones grow in the womb of a woman with child". On the other hand, *ruah* can mean spirit or life, in which case the Good News Bible gives us a neat paraphrase when it points to our inability to "understand how new life begins in the womb of a pregnant woman". Accept, says Koheleth, that there are things in human experience that we do not know; things like the mystery of birth (or of the wind and birth). Neither can we claim to know "the work of God who makes everything".

If we are going to wait until we are absolutely sure as to what God wants us to do and exactly when he wants us to do it, we are going to wait for a long time. That is no excuse for sitting around doing nothing now. Do not be like that farmer waiting for the wind to change. Get out and sow your seed in the morning and in the evening (v. 6). In other words, get cracking, redouble your efforts: you cannot guarantee results, but you increase your chances if you are diligent and make the most of the chances that come your way. There is nothing more sad than looking back on life and seeing it as a series of missed opportunities and thinking, 'If only I had done that'. Do what you have to do, do what you can do—now.

This is sound common sense in terms of our daily living. It is also a truth from which we sometimes shy away in terms of our faith. It is only too easy to separate faith from obedience. We can convince ourselves that we have real difficulty in believing certain things about God, when in fact the root of the problem lies in ourselves. The nineteenth century Scottish preacher and writer, George Macdonald, put it this way:

"Instead of asking yourself whether you believe or no, ask yourself whether you have this day done one thing because He said *Do it,* or once abstained because He said, *Do not do it.* It is surely absurd to say you believe or even want to believe in Him, if you do not do anything He tells you".

CELEBRATE LIFE

Ecclesiastes 11:7–10

[7]Light is sweet, and it is pleasant for the eyes to behold the sun.

[8]For if a man lives many years, let him rejoice in them all; but let him remember that the days of darkness will be many. All that comes is vanity.

[9]Rejoice, O young man, in your youth, and let your heart cheer you in the days of your youth; walk in the ways of your heart and the sight of your eyes. But know that for all these things God will bring you into judgment.

[10]Remove vexation from your mind, and put away pain from your body; for youth and the dawn of life are vanity.

Koheleth has been reminding us that there is much we do not know, many questions to which we have no answers. There is, however, one thing that we do know: life itself, life "the light" which he describes as "sweet" and "pleasant". For this life, says Koheleth, we ought to be grateful, grateful for every year we live, no matter how long our life may be.

There's night and day, brother, both sweet things; sun, moon and stars, brother, all sweet things; there's likewise a wind on the heath. Life is very sweet, brother; who would wish to die?

If there is a touch of romanticism in these words of George Burrow, there is none in Koheleth. Who would wish to die? Koheleth does not ask that question, he simply states as a fact, an inescapable fact, that however sweet life may be there are coming "days of darkness" which will last much longer than any days of light granted to us here on earth. Grasp the sweetness of life, says Koheleth, as long as it lasts, for death must come with all the empty meaninglessness—*hebel*—that it brings with it.

In the light of this he has a piece of advice for the young (vv.9–10). Make the most of your youth; enjoy it, "walk in the ways of your heart and the sight of your eyes". This is not an invitation to gratify every passion or to follow the lead of your roving eye. The "heart" of which he speaks is very much the mind that ensures self control, and the "sight of your eyes" is that shrewd assessment of life that he would expect every sensible person to have. Nor must we misunderstand his final comment in verse 9 that "for all these things God will bring you into judgment". It is hardly likely that Koheleth is here thinking of any final judgment beyond this present life. Rather he is insisting that what we do with our life here and now matters to God, that he will hold us responsible for the way in which we handle his gift to us. If young people do not make the most of their youth, God will want to know why.

Running through all of this is a very positive approach to life. Koheleth does not want youth spoiled by "vexation of the mind", needless worry or despair, or by "pain of the body" (*ie* the troubles that the body can bring, possibly a quiet word of warning against senseless dissipation). There is a Rabbinic saying: "Don't worry about tomorrow's worries. You do not know what a day will bring forth. Perhaps tomorrow you will not exist, so you will have been worrying about what for you may never exist". Why then spoil something which, however sweet, is all too short? Youth and "the dawn of life" or perhaps "the prime of life" (NEB) cannot last. This is but another example of *hebel*. The same mood is reflected in Shakespeare's song from *Twelfth Night:*

> What is love? 'Tis not hereafter:
> Present mirth hath present laughter;
>   What's to come is still unsure.
> In delay there lies no plenty;
> Then come kiss me sweet and twenty,
>   Youth's a stuff will not endure.

"Youth's a stuff will not endure" ... "What's to come is still unsure". Neither Shakespeare nor Koheleth intended such words to be melancholy or regretful words. Rather they are a challenge to live today to the full, accepting gratefully the opportunities it brings. Jesus invites us to take such a positive attitude towards the 'now' of our lives into the wider context of the service of the kingdom of a God who knows our every need: "So do not be anxious about tomorrow, tomorrow will look after itself. Each day has troubles enough of its own" (Matt. 6:34, NEB).

JOURNEY'S END

Ecclesiastes 12:1–8

[1]Remember also your Creator in the days of your youth, before the evil days come, and the years draw nigh, when you will say, "I have no pleasure in them"; [2]before the sun and the light and the moon and the stars are darkened and the clouds return after the rain; [3]in the day when the keepers of the house tremble, and the strong men are bent, and the grinders cease because they are few, and those that look through the windows are dimmed, [4]and the doors on the street are shut; when the sound of the grinding is low, and one rises up at the voice of a bird, and all the daughters of song are brought low; [5]they are afraid also of what is high, and terrors are in the way; the almond tree blossoms, the grasshopper drags itself along and desire fails; because man goes to his eternal home, and the mourners go about the streets; [6]before the silver cord is snapped, or the golden bowl is broken, or the pitcher is broken at the fountain, or the wheel broken at the cistern, [7]and the dust returns to the earth as it was, and the spirit returns to God who gave it. [8]Vanity of vanities, says the Preacher; all is vanity.

There are few passages in all literature which give a more moving and more vivid picture of old age and approaching death than this passage. Like much Hebrew poetry it gains its effect by placing side by side a succession of delicately sketched vignettes which together contribute to one rich picture. It is a passage, however, which has suffered at the hands of translators and commentators who have insisted on taking each of the sketches and giving them one consistent allegorical meaning by finding in them references to different parts of the human body. This approach is regrettably reflected in the Good News Bible's translation of verse 3, where that graphic sketch of a once busy and prosperous mansion now falling into decay, has disappeared. The "keepers of the house" become "your arms"; others following the same line have suggested the knees or the loins. The "strong men" become "your legs"; others have suggested the arms. The "grinders" become, not surprisingly, "the teeth", and "those that look through the windows" become "the eyes". In the same way you may explain the sun in verse 2 as the forehead or the face, the moon as the brow or the cheek, the stars as the eyeball, and the rain cloud that never passes away (GNB) as 'a bad attack of influenza accompanied by never ceasing snuffling'. This is needlessly to destroy the poetic beauty of the passage in the interests of finding one key which will unlock the door to the interpretation of all the verses. The fact that the key has to be cut differently by those who pursue this line is the least of the problems in this approach. Let us work on the assumption that the approach to the passage reflected in the RSV and the New English Bible is basically correct.

If the previous section has been an invitation to celebrate life and youth while they last, this passage begins with the call, "Remember also your Creator in the days of your youth". This is the only occasion on which Koheleth uses the word "Creator" as a description of God. This is one of the reasons why some scholars think that instead of "your Creator" we should read a very similar sounding Hebrew word meaning 'your grave'. This would make good sense in the light of what Koheleth has said elsewhere about the troubling certainty of death; but the change is hardly necessary. The passage begins in verse 1 and ends in verse 7 with the picture of man as part of the created world; fragile man who according to Genesis 2:7 is made of the dust of the earth and receives the gift of life from God; man who one day returns to the earth when God takes the gift he gave (see comment on 3:19ff.). Celebrate life, says Koheleth, but remember you only have it on temporary loan. Don't pretend that you are self-made or self-sufficient; you have a creator. Time will pass, youth and the prime of life will go, and the years will come when you will say, "I have no pleasure in them". The word here translated "pleasure" or "purpose" (NEB), is the word that occurs at the beginning of that rich tapestry of life's experiences in 3:1–9. There the RSV speaks about a time for every "matter", the New English Bible for every "activity". What is being said here is that there is coming a time when all the experiences which make life rich, all its activities, will no longer be ours to enjoy. The passing years and finally death take their toll.

So we come to Koheleth's delicately sketched vignettes of old age.

(a) The *first* picture in verse 2 is that of a gathering storm, with heavy rain clouds blotting out the light of the sun, moon and stars. This is a persistent storm that refuses to go away. No use longing for the skies to clear; even after the downpour the clouds return. It is a natural picture for Koheleth to use. He has already used "light" and the sight of the sun (11:7) as descriptions of life in all its sweetness and richness. Over against that he places "the days of darkness" and the gloomy, louring storm clouds.

(b) The *second* picture in verses 3–4 is that of a large, once busy estate falling into decay. In its heyday it was a hive of activity. There were the men—"the keepers of the house"— probably the household servants or slaves, responsible for the smooth running of the family home; "the strong men", probably the lord of the manor and his sons, living it up in style. There were the women: the slave women, busy about their menial and heavy tasks, grinding the corn; the ladies of the house spending their days looking out of the windows, leisurely noting everything that was going on. The gates were open daily as people came or went, or paid their social calls. But now the gates are closed. Hard times have come. The lords and ladies have no longer any strength for, or show any interest in, the social round. The servants are few and old. The bustle is stilled. Silence has descended. Even the bird songs are hushed (this seems to be the meaning of the second half of v. 4 where the text at points is very uncertain). The old ways, the old life; it is all dead and gone. You can get something of the same feeling today when you go into one of our large country mansions, now little more than a museum piece. The portraits are still there on the walls, but the laughter and the passions that once filled the rooms are gone. The great staircase is there, but gone are the elegantly dressed lords and ladies ascending to the ballroom. The kitchen is there with its huge spit and highly polished copper pans, but no pig is turning on the spit, no servants are scurrying around preparing the meal. The life, life both upstairs and downstairs, has gone.

(c) The *third* picture in verse 5 is that of an old man, feeble limbed, no longer able to climb a hill, a man for whom even a stroll along the street is a thought. He might stumble and break a leg or hip. The second half of the verse has three phrases describing this old man, phrases which have been variously interpreted: (1) "The almond tree blossoms". When the almond tree comes into full bloom it is covered with a delicate, pale, whitish-pink blossom. This then could be a description of an old man with a shock of white hair. Hence the Good News Bible renders, "Your hair will turn white". The same words, however, might be translated, "he despises wakefulness" (for the link between the Hebrew word for the almond tree and wakefulness, see reference to 1:11–12 in my commentary on Jeremiah in this series). This has been taken to mean that here is a feeble old man who cannot help dozing off. You can also give it a sexual meaning. Here is a man for whom sexual desire is long past. All he can do is fall asleep. (2) "The grasshopper drags itself along". The grasshopper or locust normally flits easily and swiftly from point to point. Here is a locust so heavy with over eating that it can hardly move; an appropriate image of the laboured slow movements of an old man who has difficulty in shuffling about. The word used for locust, however, is similar in sound to the Hebrew word for 'making love'. The words could thus describe an old man who had lost all vigour, a man for whom making love could only be a burden (see RSV footnote). (3) "And desire fails", or more literally, as in the New English Bible, "and caper-buds have no more zest". The caper-berry, which grows on a small shrub, was believed to have certain stimulative effects. It was thus taken as an aphrodisiac. But even this no longer has any effect. Desire has gone and cannot be reawakened.

The journey is nearing its end. Death strikes. The professional mourners are summoned to what for them is merely another job.

A man goes to "his eternal home", a natural description of what lies beyond death which occurs in many languages. For example, a seventeenth century poet, Edmund Waller, uses it, and in other respects paints a picture rather like that of Koheleth:

> The soul's dark cottage, batter'd and decay'd
> Lets in new light through chinks that time has made;
> Stronger by weakness, wiser men become,
> As they draw near to their eternal home.

Koheleth would accept the dark cottage, "batter'd and decay'd", but he has no sense of any light coming in through the chinks, no thought of strength or wisdom in this weakness. Death is a dark and cheerless end. "An eternal home" is a fitting description only because you are going to be a long time dead (see 11:8).

Two simple, yet vivid, pictures in verse 6 stress the finality of death. Both may have as their background the lordly manor and estate described in verses 3–4. The *first* is that of an expensive golden bowl or lamp, suspended from the ceiling by a silver chain. A link in the chain snaps or is removed; the golden lamp falls, to lie smashed on the floor. The *second* is that of the well in the estate. To it the women used to come every day to fill their pitchers with water drawn from the depths of the well by a pulley worked on a wheel. Now there lies beside the well only a broken pitcher and a broken wheel. To change the metaphor, the thread of life has snapped. There is no more to be said. In the end we are back (v. 7) to the beginning as described in Genesis chapter 2; the dust returns to the earth, the life to God. And in the end Koheleth is back (v. 8) where he began: "Vanity of vanities . . . all is vanity" (see comment on 1:2).

It is likely that verse 8 marks the end of the book Koheleth wrote. It would be an appropriate ending. In the few verses that remain we no longer hear Koheleth speaking to us; no more "I said" or "I saw" or "I turned to consider". There is only an assessment of Koheleth as a teacher (vv. 9–12), and a final parting shot (vv. 13–14), both probably by other hands.

FOR THE DEFENCE

Ecclesiastes 12:9–12

> [9]Besides being wise, the Preacher also taught the people knowledge, weighing and studying and arranging proverbs with great care. [10]The Preacher sought to find pleasing words, and uprightly he wrote words of truth.
>
> [11]The sayings of the wise are like goads, and like nails firmly fixed are the collected sayings which are given by one Shepherd. [12]My son, beware of anything beyond these. Of making many books there is no end, and much study is a weariness of the flesh.

It would be very surprising if some of the things Koheleth said had not given offence. To those who have all the answers, the sceptic is an irritant. To those who have a calm, untroubled faith, any doubts expressed about the claims of that faith tend to be regarded with hostility. These verses make most sense as the words of a friend or a student of Koheleth, setting out to answer attacks that have been made on his teacher. He defends him on two grounds:

(a) Koheleth, he claims, is a wisdom teacher who has thought long and hard about what he had to say. His purpose was to "[teach] people knowledge", to help them to face life honestly and intelligently. What he taught was the result of a careful sifting of the evidence; he had been "weighing and studying and arranging proverbs with great care". His concern was to make people face "the honest truth" (v. 10, NEB) about themselves and their experience. It is almost as if the readers are being challenged to be equally honest if they disagree with Koheleth. And that challenge still remains for us.

(b) Here is a man who tried to put over his teaching attractively—"he sought to find pleasing words" (v.10). "Pleasing words" could refer either to the felicitous language he used, or it could refer to the content of what he said. He did not set out to upset people; he "chose his words to give pleasure" (NEB). We do not usually win people over to our point of view or our faith by deliberately setting out to attack or upset them. Of this, Jesus is the supreme master. He did not harangue a man about his duty to other people, he told the story of the Good Samaritan (Luke 10:29ff.). He didn't preach a theology of unconditional forgiving love, he told the story of a loving father and two sons (Luke 15:11ff.). No, instead of upsetting people, we need to attract them, to interest them, to make them think for themselves.

Does Koheleth cause you offence? Then face the fact, says this man, that he does so because he is telling the honest truth, and the truth is often uncomfortable. It is not the function of the wise to leave you undisturbed in your prejudices. The words of the wise are like "goads" (v. 11), there to spur you on, to dig into you; like "nails driven home" (NEB). Hurtful, maybe, but necessary for your own good. It is true, isn't it, that we spend a lot of time and energy trying to avoid being hurt. The person to whom we find it easiest often to pretend is ourself. We blame other people. It is all their fault: they are being unreasonable. We need to be drawn up sharply in our tracks, before the truth can strike home.

And it is God's purpose to face us with the disturbing truth. The sayings of the wise (v. 11) are described as "collected sayings which are given by one Shepherd", the one Shepherd being in all probability God (cf. GNB), the source of all true wisdom. The meaning of the phrase translated "collected sayings" is far from clear. Jewish tradition tended to see in it a reference to the councils of scholars. It could refer either to a gathering of teachers, or to a gathering of those being taught, hence the New English Bible's "the assembled people", or, as in the RSV, it could refer to a gathering of what was taught, *ie* "collected sayings". Whatever it is, the argument for the defence insists that what Koheleth had to say was not only the honest truth, but it came from God.

A WARNING SHOT

Ecclesiastes 12:12–14

> 12My son, beware of anything beyond these. Of making many books there is no end, and much study is a weariness of the flesh.

¹³The end of the matter; all has been heard. Fear God, and keep his commandments; for this is the whole duty of man. ¹⁴For God will bring every deed into judgment with every secret thing, whether good or evil.

If there were some who were willing to rush to the defence of Koheleth, there were others who were less convinced and who at the very least believed that what he had been saying should be put in the context of the faith of the community as a whole. It is such a voice that we hear in the last three verses. He adopts the role of a typical wisdom teacher, addressing his audience as "My son" (see Prov. 1:8; 2:1, *etc*). He issues a blunt warning, not (as in the RSV) to beware of anything beyond "these" (*ie* the words of the wise), but instead (see NEB, GNB) about something in addition to these, namely that "of the making of books there is no end" (v. 12), *ie* don't believe everything you read. What would he have said about our world today in which in Great Britain alone one new book is published every ten minutes of every day? It is maybe not so much the writing of new books that worries him as "the use of books" (NEB). He is not advising us against reading books, but he is warning us that there is no guarantee that the number of books you read (or write) will bear any relationship to a true understanding of what life is all about.

There is more to life than study, study which at times can be frustrating or 'wearisome'. There is more to life than seeking; there must be finding. There is more to discipleship than sitting in an armchair reading a sound book on theology or a challenging book on discipleship. There must be commitment which flows out into action. So we come to what in this later commentator's view is the only thing left to say, "the end of the matter": "Fear God and keep his commandments".

Nothing could be more central to the faith of the post-exilic Hebrew community than this. Here is the recipe for a simple faith and the good life. God's commandments are there for the community to keep, written for them in *Torah*, the Law. As Psalm 119 puts it:

Lord, you have given us your laws
  and told us to obey them faithfully.
How I hope that I shall be faithful
  in keeping your instructions!
If I pay attention to all your commands,
  then I will not be put to shame.

(Ps. 119:4–6, GNB)

To act otherwise is not to fear the Lord. To fear God means to put God at the centre of life and thus to see all our own desires, hopes and ambitions in a larger context. It is to realize that all our life, everything we do or say, good or evil, is to God an open book, and he will pass his verdict. This is not a thought intended to strike terror into us. Quite the opposite. It assures us that we are dealing with a God who cares what we do; therefore life has meaning.

There is a certain irony in this concluding section if it comes from a man who is trying to redress the balance and to put Koheleth's words into a more acceptable framework. The irony lies in this; that Koheleth *could* have written these words, but they would have had a rather different meaning. As we have seen (see comment on 3:14), the fear of God can mean many different things. It could describe Koheleth bowing down before a distant God whose intentions he could not fathom, a God whom he would nevertheless take care not to offend needlessly; so he would keep the commandments. As for the last verse, it might mean no more than that we, and all we do, are obviously under God's control. He will pass his judgment on us, but whether that judgment will be good or evil, favourable or adverse—who knows? (See 9:1.)

This should remind us that when people use the same words, not least in religious circles, they do not necessarily mean the same thing. Even—perhaps most of all—the word 'God' can mean very different things to different people. That is why in the long run, it is not enough to say we believe in God. What kind of God do we believe in? To answer that as Christians, we must say not that Jesus is like God, but that God is like Jesus. That is to put a warmth and a richness into the word God of which Koheleth, as far as we can see, knew nothing.

The Book of Ecclesiastes is one of the five *Megilloth,* or Scrolls, which came to be associated in tradition with the five major festivals of the Jewish religious year. Ecclesiastes became prescribed reading on the third day of the Feast of Tabernacles, the great harvest thanksgiving festival when the dominant mood in the mind of the worshippers is one of rejoicing:

> You shall rejoice in your feast, you and your son and your daughter, your manservant and your maidservant, the Levite, the sojourner, the fatherless, and the widow who are within your towns. For seven days you shall keep the feast to the Lord your God at the place which the Lord will choose; because the Lord your God will bless you in all your produce and in all the work of your hands, so that you will be altogether joyful.
>
> (Deut. 16:14–16)

It is easy to see the link-up here with the man who says, "There is nothing better for a man than that he should eat and drink and find enjoyment in his toil", (2:24, RSV). But what about the emphasis upon "vanity", *hebel,* meaninglessness?

"Perhaps", says a Jewish writer, "it was to strike the balance of sanity that the Fathers of the Synagogue chose the recitation of Ecclesiastes with its melancholy refrain, 'Vanity of vanities, all is vanity', on the Feast of Tabernacles when the Jewish community is commanded to rejoice. At all events it is hard to escape the judgment that the major emphasis of Jewish thinking has indeed been that of setting our shoulder joyously to the world's wheel. That we have spared ourselves some unhappiness by beforehand slipping the Book of Ecclesiastes under our arm, seems likewise true".

To have the Book of Ecclesiastes in the Bible is at least to be reminded that it is possible to rejoice, to rejoice in the richness of the life God has given us, and yet live with many questions unanswered, both about life itself in this world and about the life hereafter.

SONG OF SOLOMON

INTRODUCTION

The Hebrew title of this book—"Song of Songs"—is a Hebrew
way of talking about "the finest song", just as "king of kings"
means the greatest king, and "the holy of holies" the most holy
place in the Temple. Indeed "Song of Songs" would be one way in
Hebrew of saying 'Top of the Pops'.

But in what sense can this book be called "the finest song"?
Does it have any religious value, and if so, what? Read it through
from beginning to end in a modern translation such as the Good
News Bible—it won't take you long—and you will find a lot about
"kisses", "breasts", "lips", "love", but not a single mention of
God. A collection of love poems perhaps . . . but Holy Scripture?
From an early time, doubts were being expressed as to whether
this book should be part of the Bible. There were not lacking,
however, those willing to rush to its defence. One famous Jewish
Rabbi, Akiba, claimed that, "The whole world is not worth the
day on which the Song of Songs was given to Israel; for all the
Scriptures are holy, but the Song of Songs is the Holy of Holies".
Nearly 1200 years later, Bernard of Clairvaux was in substantial
agreement with this verdict since he preached 86 sermons on the
first two chapters. No book in the Bible has been subject to more
varied assessments as to its worth, or as to how we ought to
understand it. For that reason we must pay a little more attention
than usual to such issues in this introduction.

AN ALLEGORY?

Among those who have valued the book most highly in both
Jewish and Christian circles there has been a tendency to give the

93

book an allegorical interpretation. That is to say, behind what seems to be the plain, surface meaning of the book, the celebration of human love, there lies a deeper spiritual meaning, which is its true meaning. In Jewish tradition, the bridegroom and the bride who address each other in the book are none other than God and Israel. The love they celebrate is the covenant relationship which binds God and Israel together. In Christian tradition, the book becomes the story of Christ and the Church, or Christ and the human soul. In the third century of the Christian era the great biblical scholar Origen of Alexandria in Egypt found in the Song four characters: the bridegroom who is Christ; the bride who is the Church; the friends of the bridegroom who are either angels or the prophets or the patriarchs of old; and the friends of the bride who stand for the souls of believers.

Origen was well aware, however, that this was not an interpretation which would be obvious to everyone. As some of the Jewish Rabbis before him had done, he warned that this was not a book to put into the hands of everyone. It could be so easily misunderstood. "I advise and counsel everyone who is not yet rid of the vexations of the flesh and blood and has not ceased to feel the passions of this bodily nature, to refrain from reading the book and the things that will be said about it". To guard against such misunderstanding, every detail of the book was pressed into service to provide spiritual guidance, and very different guidance could be gleaned from the same detail. Take the reference to "doves" in 1:15. Since the dove was a bird noted for its fidelity to its mate, Origen took this to refer to the Church faithful to Christ and mourning for him when he is absent. Bernard of Clairvaux, however, stressed the solitary retiring habits of the dove and used the text to encourage Christians to sit solitary and have nothing to do with the world's crowds. Even John Calvin, who was not normally given to finding allegorical meaning in Scripture, felt that this was the only way to handle this book.

Although the allegorical approach still has its advocates, it suffers from certain serious defects.

(a) It is true that the marriage relationship is used elsewhere in the Old Testament, as one of the ways of describing the relationship between God and his people Israel. A glance at Hosea chapter 2 is enough to show this. Furthermore, some of the words used to describe the bridegroom, *eg* "king" (1:4) and the shepherd who "pastures his flock" (2:16), are common titles for God in the Old Testament. Nowhere else, however, in the Old Testament is there anything remotely like the detailed development of the man–woman relationship which marks this book, with its lingering upon romantic detail and its frank and passionate sexuality. Where else do we find God speaking of Israel in the following terms (see 7:1–3, NEB)?

> How beautiful are your sandalled feet, O prince's daughter!
> The curves of your thighs are like jewels,
> the work of a skilled craftsman.
> Your navel is a rounded goblet
> that shall never want for spiced wine.
> Your belly is a heap of wheat
> fenced in by lilies.
> Your two breasts are like two fawns,
> twin fawns of a gazelle.

Or Israel addressing God (5:10–12, NEB):

> My beloved is fair and ruddy,
> a paragon among ten thousand.
> His head is gold, finest gold;
> his locks are like palm-fronds.
> His eyes are like doves beside brooks of water,
> splashed by the milky water
> as they sit where it is drawn.

To treat such language as an allegory of God and Israel, or of Christ and the Church, is to rob it of its poetry and its passion.

(b) There are usually certain clues which point us clearly to the fact that a book, or a passage in a book, is intended to be read as an allegory. For instance the names of the people and the places in an allegory very often point to the real meaning of the story. Thus John Bunyan's *Pilgrim's Progress* is about Mr Christian. Along the way he meets people like Mr Worldy Wise and Giant Despair; he comes to places like the Slough of Despond. Or think of a modern allegorical play which features Prince E. Nuff who visits Trash Town. But the people in this book have no such names, and the places referred to, like Jerusalem and Tirzah (6:4), or Heshbon, Lebanon, Damascus and Mount Carmel (7:4–5), can be found on any map of this region of the ancient Near East. So many marks of a typical allegory are missing from this book that it is hard to believe that it was written as an allegory, and it is always a dangerous game to give an allegorical interpretation to something which was not intended as an allegory. Given the absence of such clues as to how to approach it as an allegory, the book has too easily become a happy hunting ground for those who wish to read into it their own spiritual views, for reasons that have nothing at all to do with the Song of Solomon.

Many who would reject a full allegorical interpretation which seeks to discover hidden spiritual meaning in every detail of the book would nevertheless regard it as an example of *typology*. Such an approach does not deny that the book is about real people and human love, but it would see such love and the relationship it establishes as a type or pattern of something else to which it is pointing. Thus in Isaiah chapters 40–55 the prophet thinks of the coming deliverance of his people from captivity in Babylon in terms of a new Exodus (see *eg* Isa. 51:9–11; 52:11). The first Exodus from Egypt which happened hundreds of years before his time provides the prophet with a model in terms of which he can understand the way the same God is acting in his own day. This is one of the ways in which the New Testament handles the Old Testament. In Romans 5:14 Paul speaks of Adam as "a type of the one who was to come", namely Jesus.

So the human love which the Song of Solomon celebrates has been taken as a "type" of the love of God, either for Israel within Jewish tradition, or for the Church or the human soul within Christian tradition. There is, as we shall see, an element of truth in this; but typology can also be a dangerous game. How far do you push it? Is it right, for example, to take the words of 4:7— "You are all fair, my love; there is no flaw in you"—and see them as pointing forward to the Virgin Mary and the Immaculate Conception, or is this a purely arbitrary reading of a text which was never intended thus to be read? Once you begin interpreting particular verses or words in the book in this way, it is hard to see much difference in practice between typology and allegory.

A DRAMA?

Another approach to the book has been to see it as a drama. But a drama usually has a fairly clearly defined plot, in which the relationship between the leading characters changes and develops. In all great drama there is a sense of a beginning, a middle, and an ending. It is hard to get this impression from the Song of Solomon. If it is a drama, how many leading characters are there in it? Some have seen only two; King Solomon and a country girl from Shulem (6:13). Others have found three. It then becomes a story about this girl from Shulem who is deeply in love with her local shepherd lad. Along comes Solomon to drag her off to his royal harem in Jerusalem. In spite of Solomon's blandishments, however, she remains true to her shepherd love. In the end, true love triumphs and she is reunited with her village beau.

The drama would thus celebrate human love as not only the most powerful but the most holy of human emotions. It would speak to us of the joy that comes to those who are faithful, but which is denied to the sensuous. It could even be regarded as a barbed dig at Solomon with his 700 wives and 300 concubines (1 Kings 11:3). This may seem an attractive approach, but is this the plot which we sense when we read the book? I doubt it. You have got to do a great deal of reading between the lines, as well as some reordering of the text even to get a whiff of it. There are certain modern plays which on first acquaintance seem puzzling and formless, but the Song of Solomon seems even more so, and it does not have the excuse of being modern experimental theatre.

It has also been argued that the Song of Solomon is to be understood as a *cultic drama* or liturgy, celebrating the union of a god and goddess of fertility; which god and goddess depends upon whether we trace it back to Babylonian or Canaanite sources. The book is thus concerned with the recurring triumph of the forces of life over death, the annual victory of fertility over barrenness,

upon which the continuing well-being of an essentially agri-
cultural community depended. Since the king played the role of
the god when this liturgical drama was enacted in the Temple, this
accounts for the appearance of Solomon in the poems and indeed
the traditional linking of the entire book with Solomon. The
typical emphasis in such a cultic drama is, however, on the sexual
act and the concept of fertility. This is not central to the Song of
Solomon. It is not divine love, but *human* love and its longings
and its fulfilment, its fears and its delights, which is described with
a wealth of detail and poetic charm in this book. There is moreover no real evidence that a cultic drama of this pagan type was
ever part of worship in the Jerusalem Temple, even in its worst
days of apostasy.

A COLLECTION OF LOVE POEMS?

Whatever devious routes we explore, we eventually come back to
read the Song of Solomon as a collection of love poems. Love
poetry is part of the literature of all societies. We have examples
from ancient Mesopotamia and Egypt, from Greece and Rome,
from the Middle Ages, from John Donne, Robert Burns and
countless other poets down to the present day. It is not surprising
that ancient Israel makes its contribution to this perennial theme.
It may be that the book is an anthology of Hebrew love poems,
some of which may go back to the time of Solomon, others of
which may be centuries later. There have been attempts to understand the book as a collection of wedding songs. This is reflected
in the New English Bible which divides the text into passages
attributed to the "Bride", and others attributed to the "Bridegroom". Links have also been found with funeral feasts, at which
love and life are defiantly affirmed in the face of death. While
such approaches may help to explain some features in the book,
they do not adequately explain all of it. It is better to think purely
of love poems—the work, I believe, essentially of one poet—
drawing upon a rich variety of material to communicate his (or
is it her?) understanding of human love. You have only to look
at different commentaries to realise that the general stance

we adopt profoundly influences the way we interpret individual verses and words within the book. If the approach adopted here is not convincing to you, look elsewhere.

If the Song of Solomon is essentially a collection of love poems, then inevitably we must again raise the question, 'Why does such a collection of love poems appear in the Bible?'. I want to suggest that you should come back to this question after you have studied the book. Only then, in the light of the overall impression that the book has made upon you, are you in a position to answer it with any degree of conviction.

Let us at this point simply remember one thing. The link with Solomon places the book firmly along with the Book of Proverbs within the 'wisdom' tradition in ancient Israel. The distinction that we tend to make between the sacred and the secular, the religious and the non-religious, would have been quite meaningless to the wise men in Israel. The whole of life, its foibles and its strengths, the attitudes that led to success and to failure, the rich variety of human emotions, the demands made by the different relationships in which we find ourselves in life, all of these lay within their remit as they sought to give wise and helpful advice born out of experience and shrewd observation. It is not surprising, therefore, that they frequently comment on the relationship between men and women. The Song of Solomon is not the only Wisdom book to deal with this theme. Proverbs also draws attention to the dangerous sexual entanglements which can play havoc with a man's life (*eg* Provs. 6:20ff.) and neatly balances the many warnings it gives about women with its picture of the blessings that come from a capable wife (Provs. 31:10ff.). Other wisdom books, such as Ecclesiasticus, show a similar interest in sexual relationships (*eg* Ecclesiasticus 9:1–9):

Many have been misled by a woman's beauty,
and by it passion is kindled like a fire.   (Ecclesiasticus 9:8)

It is, therefore, hardly surprising that one book, standing within this tradition, should explore this relationship more fully. Where Song of Solomon differs, and differs most interestingly, is that in it we hear not only the voice of the male partner in this relationship, but the voice of the woman. Indeed within the book more verses are attributed to the woman than to the man. Is this a welcome counter-balance to the male chauvinism which often seems to speak in the biblical text?

Before we begin our study of the book, two general words of caution may be in order:

(a) The experience of human love may be timeless and universal, but the language which is thought appropriate to express it may differ widely from society to society. Sometimes we read ancient love poems and we find the ideas similar to those with which we are familiar today. We, for example, talk about 'love sickness'. So does an ancient Egyptian love poem:

> I will lie down inside,
> 　　and there I will feign illness.
> Then my neighbours will enter to see,
> 　　and then my sister [*ie* my lover] will come with them.
> She'll put the doctor to shame,
> 　　for she will understand my illness.

So in the Song of Solomon the girl asks her companions to go and find her lover and tell him, "I am sick with love" (5:8). I doubt, however, whether a bright, attractive, young girl of today would be flattered if her boyfriend sent her a Valentine card with the following words inscribed on it:

> Your hair is like a flock of goats,
> 　　moving down the slopes of Gilead.
> Your teeth are like a flock of ewes,
> 　　that have come up from the washing,
> all of them bear twins,
> 　　not one of them is bereaved.
> Your cheeks are like halves of a pomegranate
> 　　behind your veil.　　　　　　　　　　　　　　(6:5*b*–8)

Nor would he feel particularly romantic if back came the reply:

> His cheeks are like beds of spices,
> 　　yielding fragrance.
> His lips are lilies,
> 　　distilling liquid myrrh.

His arms are rounded gold,
    set with jewels.
His body is ivory work,
    encrusted with sapphires.
His legs are alabaster columns,
    set upon bases of gold.
His appearance is like Lebanon,
    choice as the cedars. (5:13–15)

We would settle more happily for:

O My luve's like a red, red rose,
    That's newly sprung in June:
O My luve's like the melodie,
    That's sweetly play'd in tune.

(Robert Burns)

We have to do a good deal of translating into our own ways of thinking before we can appreciate the passionate but alien tenderness, the swiftly changing moods and emotions, which speak to us in the Song of Solomon.

The same holds true for the meaning of many words and phrases in the book. Words occur in the Song of Solomon which are to be found nowhere else in the Old Testament; and words which mean one thing in other parts of the Old Testament obviously have a different meaning in this book. It is good that we should be aware of these problems. Sometimes we can only guess at the meaning of words; and no-one should claim infallibility for such guesses.

(b) There is little doubt that in the Song of Solomon we are listening to different voices, *at least* two—a woman and a man. But how do we divide the poems between these voices? Sometimes the division is obvious, but by no means always. Again, what role is played by "the daughters of Jerusalem" (2:7 *etc*)? Are any verses to be attributed to them, and if so, which ones? Most modern translations, although not the RSV, try to be helpful—as some early Greek manuscripts did—by dividing the text for you. A brief look at two passages, however, will show you that this leaves many questions unanswered.

Take first chapter 1, verses 1–11 in the New English Bible, the Good News Bible and the Jerusalem Bible:

NEB	GNB	JB
Bride 2–4*a*	The Woman 2–7	Bride 2–4, 5–7 (two speeches)
Companions 4*b* Bride 5–7		
Bridegroom 8–10	The Man 8–11	Chorus 8 Bridegroom 9–11
Companions 11		

Or take chapter 2:8–3:11

NEB	GNB	JB
Bride 2:8–13	The Woman 2:8–10*a*	Bride 2:8–3:4
Bridegroom 2:14	The Man 2:10*b*–15	
Companions 2:15		
Bride 2:16–3:4	The Woman 2:16–3:5	
Bridegroom 3:5		Bridegroom 3:5, 6–11 (two speeches)
Companions 3:6–11	The Woman 3:6–11 (a new speech)	

Behind each of these different ways of dividing the text there lie decisions as to how we are to understand it. If a certain approach is taken in this commentary, remember that it is only one of several that are possible.

LONGINGS—A WOMAN'S THOUGHTS

Song of Solomon 1:1–4

¹The Song of Songs, which is Solomon's.

²O that you would kiss me with the kisses of your mouth!
 For your love is better than wine,
³ your anointing oils are fragrant,
 your name is oil poured out;
   therefore the maidens love you.

⁴Draw me after you, let us make haste.
   The king has brought me into his chambers.
 We will exult and rejoice in you;
   we will extol your love more than wine;
   rightly do they love you.

After the heading to the book in verse 1—for which see the Introduction—we listen to the passionate longing of a girl for the joy that love will bring to her. It has been suggested that throughout the book it is a recently married couple who are sharing with us the ecstasy and the tensions of the first months of their life together. While this may be thought to tidy up the morality of some of the poems, it is highly unlikely in view of some of the language and the thoughts expressed, for example the need and desire for secret meetings.

The New English Bible catches well the sense of verse 2 when it renders, may he "smother me with kisses". Many translations try to tidy up the language for us at this point by making the girl address her lover as "you" in verse 2: thus RSV. In the original, however, verse 2 speaks of "he" and "his mouth", and only in verse 3 do we have a switch to "you". This kind of switch is quite common in Hebrew poetry and is not uncommon in love poetry from other ancient cultures. It is as if she begins by thinking about him and then almost unconsciously she is speaking to him. One moment she is thinking of her lover as someone who will come and smother her with his kisses, the next she is savouring the intensely personal relationship which can only take place between a "you" and a "me".

Wine and oil, used as basic ingredients in various types of perfume, are repeatedly associated with joy and gladness in the Old Testament (see Eccles. 9:7–8), so it is but natural that they are here associated with "love". The word used for love here in verse 2 (Hebrew *dodim*) has a strongly sexual flavour. It is used in Proverbs chapter 7 of the wife who, when her husband is away on business, spreads her favours far and wide, inviting men into her house with the words, "Come, let us make love all night long" (Prov. 7:18, GNB). So the girl longs for that love-making which will bring her greater delight than wine and for the sensual presence of her lover. Even to mention his name conjures up all kinds of delights, an experience to which lovers in all ages bear witness. His name is like "oil poured out" (v. 3). This translation assumes an alteration to the traditional Hebrew text which goes as far back as the Greek (*Septuagint*) translation. The Hebrew text could be rendered "oil of Turaq", with Turaq being presumably the name of a well known, perhaps particularly desirable or costly oil. Was "oil of Turaq" the ancient Hebrew equivalent of Brut for men?

Two people fall in love and you hear the comment, 'I wonder what she sees in him'. She of course is meanwhile wondering how anyone can fail to see all the desirable and attractive qualities that she finds in him. So this girl can only assume that the "maidens", all the other young girls, share her love for, her delight in, the one who has won her heart (vv. 3–4). Yet his love must be for her alone, so she eagerly asks him to "Draw me after you", or as the New English Bible and Good News Bibles translate, "Take me with you". The word translated "draw" in the RSV is used elsewhere in the Old Testament to describe the powerful attraction of love. The prophet Hosea speaks of God drawing his people to him with affection and love (Hos. 11:4, NEB). Here it is a human attraction which looks for its consummation in the bedroom: the "chambers" (RSV, v. 4) always refers to the private inner room, whether it be in a tent or in a more substantial building. It was there that Amnon brutally raped his sister Tamar (see 2 Sam. 13).

Notice the way in which the woman addresses her lover as "king". This is not a reference to a king such as Solomon. There is a long tradition in love poetry, which we can trace back as far as ancient Egypt, where lovers address each other as king or queen, prince or princess. We still do so today. There is many a girl still waiting for her 'Prince Charming'. Here is a modern writer using the same kind of language and explaining why it is appropriate: "When I told you that I loved you, this is what I meant by it, that you would reign like a queen in my thoughts forever . . . . Love is a kingdom where the poorest man is king".

HESITATIONS

Song of Solomon 1:5–7

> ⁵I am very dark, but comely,
>> O daughters of Jerusalem,
> like the tents of Kedar,
>> like the curtains of Solomon.
> ⁶Do not gaze at me because I am swarthy,
>> because the sun has scorched me.
> My mother's sons were angry with me,
>> they made me keeper of the vineyards;
>> but, my own vineyard I have not kept!
> ⁷Tell me, you whom my soul loves,
>> where you pasture your flock,
>> where you make it lie down at noon;
> for why should I be like one who wanders
>> beside the flocks of your companions?

Desire, urgent desire looking for fulfilment . . . yet side by side with it, as so often, there goes hesitation, rooted in this case in three factors:

(a) There is the girl's own lack of self-confidence. Is she attractive enough? "I am very dark, but comely" (vv. 5–6a), words that could just as easily be translated, 'Dark am I and attractive'. The problem here is that sometimes in ancient texts black is equated with beauty, sometimes it is regarded as the opposite of beauty which is symbolized by whiteness. In context it looks as if these words are not a claim that 'black is beautiful'. The picture is rather that of a girl, naturally fairish in complexion, who has been forced to work outside under the scorching sun, and is therefore deeply tanned. She compares herself to "the tents of Kedar". Kedar is strictly a desert region to the south-east of Damascus, but it is probably used here to indicate any of the Bedouin tribesmen whose tents are black, made out of the skins of their black goats.

The "curtains of Solomon" (v. 5) are rather more problematic. Are these "curtains of Solomon" the rich tapestries adorning the walls of the royal palace and therefore intended to be a contrast to the dark tents of Kedar, just as the girl's attractiveness is in contrast to her dark skin? The "curtains", however, might refer to the dark hangings which divided the tent into separate quarters, and thus just another way of referring to the dark tents. The New English Bible translation assumes that instead of Solomon we read Shalmah—the Hebrew letters could be read either way—Shalmah being another tribal name parallel to Kedar. This would make good sense although there is no other evidence for the name Shalmah in the Old Testament.

If the woman's complexion is tanned, dark like the desert tents, will she be less attractive to her lover than the fair skinned city girls? Verse 5 introduces for the first time the "daughters of Jerusalem" who are addressed on several occasions in the book and always by the girl (*eg* 2:7; 3:5, 10). What their role is in the poems is far from clear. Read the poems as wedding songs and they can be the companions of the bride, not least if it is a royal wedding in Jerusalem which is being celebrated. If the book is a drama then they can function as a chorus. If the girl who is declaring her love in this opening section is a country girl, the daughters of Jerusalem may represent the more sophisticated women of the capital, whom she half envies and half fears. So her self doubts come to the surface.

(b) There is the attitude of her family (v. 6*b*). The reference to "my mother's sons" and the absence of any reference in the book to her father, suggests that her father is dead. Her brothers are now responsible for the affairs of the family. If she wishes to marry, such a marriage must be formally arranged by her brothers. It looks as if the brothers are not sympathetic to her heart's desire although no reason is given at this point in the text for their anger (but see comment on 8:8–9). The Hebrew word translated "were angry with" (v. 6) comes from a verb which basically means to be hot. There is perhaps an intentional play on words. Not only did the heat of the sun spoil her chances, so did "the heat" of her family.

The brothers may have thought that she was not ready for marriage. The cure for her romantic illusions was hard work; she was sent to tend the family vineyards. Plaintively she protests "but, my own vineyard I have not kept". Like many other words in the Song of Solomon the word "vineyard" has a double meaning. When it is first used in this verse it means quite literally the vineyards owned by the family. The girl is not, however, arguing that she herself owns such a vineyard. The "vineyard" now means herself, in particular her sexuality which her lover will cultivate. The Good News Bible goes part of the way towards this when it translates, "I had no time to care for myself". Because of the demands her brothers made upon her she had not had time to develop her own love life. It is like a Cinderella story with the brothers in the role of the ugly sisters. But at least this Cinderella knows who her Prince Charming is, without going to the ball.

(c) The scene switches from the vineyard to the life of the shepherd as she explores another possible problem. If she were free to go to him, where would she find him? He is her one and only heart's desire. This is stressed in the phrase "you whom my soul loves" (v. 7); "my soul" being an emphatic way of saying 'I' often with an undertone of "my desire". The New English Bible translates this as, "my true love". But this, her true love, is a shepherd lad, grazing his flocks with the other shepherds, taking like them a noon-day siesta. But where? She can hardly go out "like one who wanders".

This is a phrase which has provoked a good deal of discussion. The RSV rendering is the result of changing the order of two of the letters in the Hebrew word. The New English Bible assumes that the word can mean "picking lice" from a garment, a common enough practice among shepherds in the East (see Jer. 43:12). It is perhaps best to take the Hebrew to mean, "a veiled woman" (NIV), the veil referred to being that worn by a prostitute soliciting business (see Gen. 38:15 where Tamar gets her legal rights from her father-in-law, Judah, by pretending to be a prostitute). You can hardly want me, she says to her lover, to go wandering around like a common harlot soliciting business among the, no doubt, all too willing shepherds, until I find you. She may be indicating quite firmly to her lover that she is not that type of girl; but there may almost be a hint of desperation in her words as if to say that she would be prepared to go to almost any lengths to find him.

WORDS OF ENCOURAGEMENT—
THE MAN'S RESPONSE

Song of Solomon 1:8–11

[8]If you do not know,
  O fairest among women,
 follow in the tracks of the flock,
  and pasture your kids
  beside the shepherds' tents.
[9]I compare you, my love,
  to a mare of Pharaoh's chariots.
[10]Your cheeks are comely with ornaments,
  your neck with strings of jewels.
[11]We will make you ornaments of gold,
  studded with silver.

How can a girl's hesitation be answered except by words of gentle reassurance? Her comments about her own attractiveness, or lack of it, are immediately countered when her lover calls her, "O fairest among women" (v. 8), or to use a rather more modern idiom, 'my pin up girl'. Perhaps her self-depreciating words were intended to evoke such a response—it has been known to happen. If so, they succeed. All of us need and respond to words of praise and encouragement especially from those we love.

The rest of verse 8 picks up the fear she voiced that she may not be able to find him. It seems to say, if you really don't know where to find me, go and ask; follow the shepherds around. The trouble with this of course is that she has just said that to do this would be to invite misunderstanding. It may be that he is gently reassuring her that this will not happen. The language of following "the tracks of the flock" and "pasture your kids", however, can have the same kind of double meaning that we found in the word "vineyard" in verse 6. The words translated "pasture" and "shepherd" in this verse have the same basic letters in Hebrew as the word translated "my love" (NEB, "my dearest") in verse 9. Thus he may be inviting her to throw caution to the wind and come in search of the love she desires.

Lest she should have any further doubts about her attractiveness or her desirability in the eyes of her lover, he proceeds in verse 9 to use a comparison, as lovers have done in all ages. We have no difficulty in understanding what Burns means when he says, "My Luve's like a red, red rose", or what Shakespeare means when he says, "Shall I compare thee to a summer's day? Thou art more lovely and more temperate". It is perhaps not so immediately obvious to us, however, what is meant when the lover compares his heart's desire to "a mare of Pharaoh's chariots" (v. 9). In the ancient world the Egyptians were noted, among other things, for their chariots. In military terms, such chariots were the equivalent of the tank corps; on more peaceful state occasions the equivalent of the Rolls Royce or the Cadillac. Such chariots were usually drawn by the finest bred stallions, the equivalent of today's thoroughbred Arabian stallions. But why compare her to "a mare of Pharaoh's chariots"? Is this purely an obvious sexual term to apply to a well bred attractive filly, or is there something more to it than this? There is at least one well documented story in Egyptian annals describing an incident during an Egyptian campaign in the Lebanon when a shrewd enemy commander tried to offset Egyptian military superiority and create havoc in the Egyptian ranks by letting loose a mare among the stallions pulling the Egyptian chariots. Something like this lies behind the Good News Bible's paraphrase (1:9):

> You, my love, excite men
>   as a mare excites the stallions of
>   Pharaoh's chariots.

This, then, is a way of referring to her irresistible sex appeal. You have the ability, he is saying, to turn any man's head.

Egyptian horses, like show horses today, were finely groomed with richly ornamented bridles and harness; so the beauty of his beloved, the beauty of her cheeks and her neck, is enhanced by the jewellery she wears and any jewellery she may be given. There is some doubt as to the precise meaning of some of the words used for ornaments and jewels in verses 10–11, but the overall picture is clear. It is not the value of such trinkets or jewels that is being stressed, only the way in which they serve to highlight the beauty the girl already has in the eyes of her lover.

WHAT IT MEANS TO BE IN LOVE

Song of Solomon 1:12–14

> [12]While the king was on his couch,
>   my nard gave forth its fragrance.
> [13]My beloved is to me a bag of myrrh,
>   that lies between my breasts.
> [14]My beloved is to me a cluster of henna blossoms
>   in the vineyards of En-gedi.

The lover's compliments are interrupted by the woman's thoughts as she savours in her mind the delights of lying in his arms, locked in a passionate embrace. (For the reference to her lover as "the king" see comment on 1:4.) She uses a series of delightfully naïve, yet powerfully erotic pictures:

(a) Her own desirability, and indeed her eagerness, are stressed in the first picture, "my nard gave forth its fragrance" (v. 12). Nard or spikenard (NEB) is a fragrant, aromatic oil derived from a plant native to the Himalayas, but widely used in the ancient Near East as a love charm. No doubt today it would feature in one of those TV commercials designed to convince us that the use of a certain spray or perfume will guarantee a romantic evening.

(b) The intimate closeness of her lover is described in the picture of him as "a bag of myrrh that lies between my breasts" (v. 13). Myrrh is the aromatic gum which comes from the bark of a tree that flourishes in Arabia. Its fragrant smell led to it being highly prized. The Book of Esther claims that the women in King Ahasuerus' harem were only admitted into the royal boudoir after an intensive year-long beauty treatment involving "six months with oil of myrrh and six months with spices and perfumes for women" (Esther 2:12). That wife of easy morals in Proverbs chapter 7 perfumed her bed with myrrh, among other equally alluring scents (Prov. 7:17). Wearing a sachet of myrrh between the breasts served the same purpose for women in ancient Israel as a dab of Chanel in the same place is supposed to do today. Here she thinks of her lover, in all his attractiveness, as being such a sachet of myrrh lying (literally 'spending the night') between her breasts.

(c) Her lover is further described as a "cluster of henna blossoms" (v. 14). The henna plant, a shrub that grows some eight to ten feet high throughout the Levant, produces a mass of bluish-yellow flowers, tightly packed together and resembling a bunch of grapes. From the dried leaves of the plant, a dye is produced and applied to hair and nails. The emphasis here, however, seems to be on the fragrant smell emanating from the flowers, a picture of the desirability of her lover. This henna blossom is said to come "from" (NEB), rather than "in" (RSV), "the vineyards of En-gedi", meaning Kid Fountain, a very fertile oasis on the west shore of the Dead Sea. It was hemmed in by towering cliffs, the haunt of wild goats. Its sheltered position, its warm springs, sustained a profusion of plants, in stark contrast to the bareness of much of the surrounding countryside.

Thus she dreams of one whom twice she calls "my beloved" (vv. 13–14). This is the same Hebrew word which in verse 2 is translated "love"; Hebrew and English, along with many other languages, using the word 'love' both for the relationship and for the other person. So we speak of 'love' and refer to someone as 'my love'.

REJOICING IN EACH OTHER

Song of Solomon 1:15–2:2

> [15]Behold, you are beautiful, my love;
>   behold, you are beautiful;
>   your eyes are doves.
> [16]Behold, you are beautiful, my beloved,
>   truly lovely.
> Our couch is green;
>   [17]the beams of our house are cedar,
>   our rafters are pine.
> [1]I am a rose of Sharon,
>   a lily of the valleys.
> [2]As a lily among brambles,
>   so is my love among maidens.

In this section the lovers exchange compliments, picking up and echoing each other's words, just as today someone might say, 'I love you' and hear the reply, 'And I love you'. The man begins in verse 15 by praising the girl's beauty, her attractiveness. "Behold, you are beautiful" or "How beautiful you are!" (GNB, NEB), my love—for 'my love' see comment on verse 9. He compares her eyes to doves. Beautiful eyes were certainly a source of attractiveness in ancient Israel (cf. the comments on Leah and Rachel in Gen. 29:17). But what is the point of the comparison to doves? The Good News Bible translates, "How your eyes shine with love". This is probably based on the glistening feathers of the dove and its quick movements, or the dove is simply being regarded as the love bird (see 2:14). Others have seen here a reference to the dove's deep smoke-grey colour or to its softness or to its gentleness. Speculation has abounded across the centuries. Although doves are to flit in and out of the book, it is hard to be certain what characteristic of the dove is intended.

The girl immediately returns the compliment in verse 16, "How beautiful you are, my beloved" (see comment on vv. 13–14) and adds for good measure "truly lovely" or attractive. Then beginning with the words "our couch" (rather "our bed"), together, or with the man speaking for both of them, they pledge their love to each other, a love to be shared under the open skies; their sole canopy the green leafy branches (not, as in the GNB, "the green grass"), and with only trees as a roof or ceiling above their head. All they need and want is each other and the freedom and privacy to share and enjoy their love.

Diffidently in 2:1 the girl describes herself as a "rose of Sharon" (NEB an "asphodel in Sharon"; GNB, "only a wild flower in Sharon"). Sharon is the coastal plain south of the Carmel range. The different English translations, however, underline the difficulty in deciding what kind of flower is intended. "Rose" is misleading. The Hebrew word seems to indicate a flower which grows from a bulb, hence RSV footnote "crocus"; iris or anemone have also been suggested. The context seems to point to some quite common and not particularly valued flower. And this applies also to the "lily of the valleys", which is not our lily of the valley, but some variety of water lily which thrives in the pools and rivers along the valleys. The girl uses the same word to describe her lover's lips in 5:13, but whether this indicates their shape or their colour we do not know. It is as if she is saying to her lover, 'I am no valuable orchid, but only a common daisy'. That may be so, says her lover in 2:2, merely a lily, yes but compared with other girls, "a lily among brambles" or "a lily among thorns" (NEB).

How true to life is this almost bantering exchange! However other people see us, whatever value we place upon ourselves, we are seen very differently through the eyes of someone who loves us.

THE SWEET FRUITS OF LOVE

Song of Solomon 2:3–7

> ³As an apple tree among the trees of the wood,
>   so is my beloved among young men.
> With great delight I sat in his shadow,
>   and his fruit was sweet to my taste.
> ⁴He brought me to the banqueting house,
>   and his banner over me was love.
> ⁵Sustain me with raisins,
>   refresh me with apples;
>   for I am sick with love.
> ⁶O that his left hand were under my head,
>   and that his right hand embraced me!
> ⁷I adjure you, O daughters of Jerusalem,
>   by the gazelles or the hinds of the field,
> that you stir not up nor awaken love until it please.

The girl's delight in her lover, her eagerness to enter more fully into a relationship with him, occupy her thoughts. She begins by expressing the joy that comes to her just being in his company. It is better to read verses 3 and 4 in the present tense rather than in the past, hence "I sit" and "his fruit is sweet" (v. 3). In verse 3 she deftly returns the compliment he has paid her. If, in his eyes, she is like a lily in the midst of thorns in comparison with other girls, then he, in her eyes, in comparison with other young men, is like "an apple tree among the trees of the wood". The word translated "apple tree", which occurs again in 7:8 and 8:5, is of uncertain meaning. Early Jewish translations rendered it as "citrus", some modern translations as "an apricot-tree" (NEB). Whatever kind of tree it is, it provides pleasant shade from the heat of the sun, and it is a tree whose fruit tastes sweet. Such is the delight she finds in the presence of her lover, as she savours the sweetness of his caresses and kisses (cf. 5:16).

The meaning of verse 4 is something of a puzzle. What is meant by "the banqueting house" to which "he brings" her (present tense), literally "the house of wine", a phrase which in this precise form occurs nowhere else in the Old Testament? "House" might indicate any kind of place, so the New English Bible renders, "wine-garden". Since their love story is being played out, so far, under the open skies with only the leafy branches of the trees above them, it is possible that the reference is to a vineyard, rather than to some kind of tavern or indoor banquet. The second half of the verse presents equal problems. In spite of the way in which hymns and choruses have fastened on the phrase, "his banner over me was [is] love", it is not clear what the phrase means, nor is there much justification for the translation "banner". The word seems strictly to mean a unit or division in an army, rather than the standard or the banner it carries. Behind the New English Bible's translation, "and gave me loving glances", which makes a good deal of sense in context, there lies the meaning 'intention' or 'desire' from a similar word found in other ancient Near Eastern languages.

The girl knows that his intentions are to make love to her; she herself makes no pretence to be anything other than "sick with love" (v. 5), a common ailment which has struck down the strongest and most rational of men and women. Not that she wants a cure, other than to lie in his arms and to feel his touch (v. 6). There has been a lot of speculation as to what the first half of verse 5 means, but there is little agreement. It has been argued that both "raisins" or "raisin cakes"—if that is what the word means—and "apples" or "apricots" (see v. 3) were thought of as sexual stimulants, but it is hard to imagine this girl needing them! It may be that she is merely appealing for sustaining food to give her strength while she waits and longs for the consummation of their love.

Verse 7, her appeal to the "daughters of Jerusalem", appears again at 3:5 and 8:4. In 8:4 it is immediately preceded by the same words as here in verse 6, and in 3:5, it follows a verse which describes the woman clinging to her lover. It may be that this verse (v. 7) is being used like the fade out scene in old fashioned movies, gently and discretely hinting at what is to follow. It is as if a couple of newlyweds enter their bedroom and ask the hotel porter to ensure that there is a notice pinned to the door saying, 'Do not disturb'. At least that is one interpretation of the last line of the verse, an interpretation neatly paraphrased by the Good News Bible's, "that you will not interrupt our love". This assumes that the word translated "stir" in the RSV means disturb.

The RSV translation, on the other hand, assumes that the girl is pleading that the others should understand the depths of her passion and that her love should be allowed to take its natural course at an appropriate time. But why does she extract a solemn oath or promise from "the daughters of Jerusalem" (see 1:5) "by the gazelles or the hinds of the field"? There is some evidence from outside the Old Testament that the gazelle was associated with sexual potency and fertility, which would provide a reason for the gazelles and the hinds of the field being invoked here.

The New English Bible's translation, "by the spirits and the goddesses of the fields", follows a tradition which goes back to some of the early translations of the Bible. The Aramaic Targum takes the word translated gazelles to be a title of God, the Lord of hosts, and it is possible to see behind the words rendered, "the hinds of the field", another title for God, normally translated "God Almighty" in the Old Testament. The Greek (*Septuagint*) text gives "by the powers and forces of the field", perhaps a reference to the local spirits of fertility. It is difficult to be sure, but it is unlikely that there is any specific reference to the God of

Israel since such references are conspicuous by their absence
elsewhere in the book.

Whatever the difficulties of the verse, the women of Jerusalem
are being used as a kind of sounding board for the girl's own
intense feelings; as if she is saying to them, 'you must know what it
is like to be in love—help me'.

DREAMING OF LOVE

Song of Solomon 2:8–17

8The voice of my beloved!
    Behold, he comes,
  leaping upon the mountains,
    bounding over the hills.
9My beloved is like a gazelle,
    or a young stag.
  Behold, there he stands
    behind our wall,
  gazing in at the windows,
    looking through the lattice.
10My beloved speaks and says to me:
  "Arise, my love, my fair one,
    and come away;
11for lo, the winter is past,
    the rain is over and gone.
12The flowers appear on the earth,
    the time of singing has come,
  and the voice of the turtledove
    is heard in our land.
13The fig tree puts forth its figs,
    and the vines are in blossom;
    they give forth fragrance.
  Arise, my love, my fair one,
    and come away.
14O my dove, in the clefts of the rock,
    in the covert of the cliff,
  let me see your face,
    let me hear your voice,
  for your voice is sweet,
    and your face is comely".

¹⁵Catch us the foxes,
   the little foxes,
  that spoil the vineyards,
   for our vineyards are in blossom.
¹⁶My beloved is mine and I am his,
   he pastures his flock among the lilies.
¹⁷Until the day breathes
   and the shadows flee,
  turn, my beloved, be like a gazelle,
   or a young stag upon rugged mountains.

In this beautiful and lyrical poem the girl dreams of her lover. It is a carefully crafted poem. At the beginning she imagines her lover swiftly coming to her, leaping over the hills "like a gazelle, or a young stag" (v. 9) and at the end he also departs "like a gazelle, or a young stag" (v. 17)—the end echoes the beginning. Three times within the poem we hear the word "Behold"—verses 8, 9 and in verse 11 where the RSV renders, "lo"—as if to stress the intense excitement which grips her. Twice—in verses 10 and 13—she hears his invitation, neatly translated in the Good News Bible:

Come then, my love;
   my darling, come with me.

Instead of taking the opening words of the poem as "The voice of my beloved", it is better to take the word "voice" also as an exclamation and to translate it as "Listen! [NEB "Hark"] My Beloved!" He comes fleet of foot. He stands outside "our wall" (v. 9). He gazes in through the window, unable to reach her, urging her to come out and join him (v. 10)

His invitation is capped by a marvellous description of the world bursting into new life in spring time (vv. 11–13), symbol of the new life which love has to offer. Winter, the rainy season which normally ends around mid-April, is past. Spring flowers appear in the countryside, like the snowdrops and aconites I saw the other day carpeting the earth under a small copse of trees. It is the time of "singing", the time of the bird songs, although the word translated singing could also mean "pruning". Since, however, pruning took place in Palestine in early autumn rather than in the spring, this would not be so appropriate here. It is the time when the migrating "turtledove" returns, usually early April. (The word translated "turtledove" is not the same word as that for the non-migrating dove of 1:15 and 2:14.) It is the time when we normally see the geese flying north. It is the time when the early figs begin to form. Compare the use that Jesus made of the same picture in Mark 13:28 (GNB), 'Let the fig tree teach you a lesson. When its branches become green and tender, and it starts putting out leaves, you know that summer is near!' For Jesus it was a sign of the times and the nearness of "the Son of Man"; for the lovers a sign of their awakening and ripening love. The vineyards too are heavy with the scent of blossom—this at least seems to be the general meaning of the difficult text in the second half of verse 13.

As her lover stands outside he cannot reach her, he cannot even see her properly, so he describes her as "my dove"; the dove a symbol of love, but a bird that timidly hides in the crevices of rock faces or the ledges of cliffs (v. 14). He may not be able to reach her, but she knows that they are one: 'My beloved is mine and I am his' (v. 16). Gladly would she be his lover. The picture of him pasturing his flock among the lilies has a sexual meaning, the lilies in all probability being her lips (cf. 5:13), unless indeed it has an even more intimate sense.

The only major puzzle in the poem is verse 15 with its reference to the little foxes which spoil or destroy the vineyards. Just as foxes raid hen farms today, so they used to cause havoc in the vineyards in ancient times. A Greek poem says:

A plague on the foxes, bushy tailed vermin that creep
To plunder the vines in the evening when Micon's asleep.

The girl may thus be pleading that nothing should be allowed to destroy the love that is blossoming between them. There may, however, be a more explicitly sexual meaning, with the little foxes representing all other eager young men, and the vineyard representing the girl's sexuality. She may be teasing her lover, playfully suggesting that he better watch out since there are others vying with him for her favours.

The poem closes with dawn breaking; "the day breathes" being a reference to the cool breeze of early morning. The shadows of the night disappear from the sky. Her lover must go. He swiftly departs like a gazelle "upon rugged mountains" (v. 17). The various approaches to the difficult closing words of the poem are well illustrated in the standard English translations. RSV's "rugged" assumes that we are dealing with a word that basically means 'divide'. The New English Bible's "on the hills where cinnamon grows" finds a link with a word for spices. The Good News Bible's "on the mountains of Bether" assumes rather weakly that we are dealing with a place name, like the mountains of Mourne in the Irish song, although the identification of the place becomes something of a guessing game.

Those who wish to give the whole book an allegorical interpretation have had a field day with this poem. Christian allegorists have found in verse 8 a reference to Christ immediately after his advent, or the voice has been taken as the call to resurrection before the Second Coming. As for leaping and bounding, this may represent Christ coming into the womb of Mary, or it may speak of his burial, leaping from the cross to the grave. Alternatively he comes leaping to us from the pages of the Bible, from the hills of the Old Testament and from the higher hills of the New Testament. One can only comment that it is sad to destroy such a delightful poem in the interests of such false and forced interpretation of Scripture. Does our faith really need this kind of support?

THE DREAM OF A LOST LOVER

Song of Solomon 3:1–5

[1]Upon my bed by night
  I sought him whom my soul loves;
 I sought him, but found him not;
  I called him, but he gave no answer.

²"I will rise now and go about the city,
    in the streets and in the squares;
 I will seek him whom my soul loves."
    I sought him, but found him not.
³The watchmen found me,
    as they went about in the city.
 "Have you seen him whom my soul loves?"
⁴Scarcely had I passed them,
    when I found him whom my soul loves.
 I held him, and would not let him go
    until I had brought him into my mother's house,
    and into the chamber of her that conceived me.
⁵I adjure you, O daughters of Jerusalem,
    by the gazelles or the hinds of the field,
 that you stir not up nor awaken love until it please.

In the poem in 2:8–17 the girl imagines her lover eagerly coming
to her. Now the roles are reversed; she dreams that she has to take
the initiative and go in search of him. Throughout this dream
there echo the words 'seeking' (twice in v. 1, twice in v. 2) and
'finding' (vv. 1–4). Four times she speaks of her lost lover as "him
whom my soul loves" (vv. 1–4; see comment on 1:7). Night after
night, lying on her bed she cannot get him out of her thoughts.
She looks for him, but he is not there; and, if we follow the Greek
text (see RSV ftn. to v. 1), she calls out to him, but gets no
answer. She imagines herself going out to search for him in the
streets and squares of the city. She asks the 'night watchmen' on
patrol whether they have seen him. What they were supposed to
think of a young girl roaming the streets at night in search of a
young man we are not told. Perhaps she imagines them regarding
her with stony indifference; that would be a charitable interpretation to place on their lack of response. Not that it matters. She
finds him; she clings to him, refusing to let him go until she has
brought him to her "mother's house" (v. 4, cf. 8:2; and see
comment on 1:6). It is not only an introduction to the family she
has in mind, however; she wishes to take her lover "into the
chamber of her that conceived me" (v. 4), or as the Good News

Bible says, "to the room where I was born". She is antici-
pating the consummation of their love in the very place where she
herself was conceived or born.

If we take the book to be the reflection of the experience of one
girl, then 8:2, which still looks forward to the day when she can
openly express her love and take her lover into "the house of [her]
mother", suggests that what we have here can only be a dream in
which she is sharing with us her longings. If on the other hand the
book is an anthology of love poems reflecting the experience of
different people, we can draw no such conclusion. Yet whoever
speaks here, look at what a mockery it makes of some of the
conventions of the society in which she was brought up, a society
in which marriage was arranged by the men at a family gathering,
where a woman's status tended to be defined by her relationship
to men, to her father and brothers *before* she was married, to her
husband *after* she was married. All such social conventions are
here transcended as she lays bare her inner soul. She will take the
initiative in going in search of her lover; she will take him home
there to consummate their love. The laws and customs of the
societies in which we live are ultimately powerless to stifle the
deepest passions that surge through our lives, whether love or the
desire for freedom, political or religious. Some of the greatest
tragedies in life and in literature have revolved around the clash
between such customs and passions—witness the tensions and
conflicts in South Africa today and the defiance of a Winnie
Mandela. (For the last verse see comment on 2:7).

A RIGHT ROYAL DAY

Song of Solomon 3:6–11

6What is that coming up from the wilderness,
    like a column of smoke,
  perfumed with myrrh and frankincense,
    with all the fragrant powders of the merchant?
7Behold, it is the litter of Solomon!
  About it are sixty mighty men
    of the mighty men of Israel,

8all girt with swords
    and expert in war,
  each with his sword at his thigh,
    against alarms by night.
9King Solomon made himself a palanquin
    from the wood of Lebanon.
10He made its posts of silver,
    its back of gold, its seat of purple;
  it was lovingly wrought within
    by the daughters of Jerusalem.
11Go forth, O daughters of Zion,
    and behold King Solomon,
  with the crown with which his mother crowned him
    on the day of his wedding,
    on the day of the gladness of his heart.

This section raises a number of questions to which there are no easy answers. It is the only section in the book in which Solomon seems to appear in his own right as a person (see vv. 7, 9, 11). Elsewhere, at 1:5 his name is merely used in a comparison, and in 8:11–12 he is no more than the foil for the girl's true lover. Further, only in this section do we have a reference to "Israel" (v. 7) and to "Zion" (v. 11). If the book is an anthology of poems coming from many different periods in the life of Israel, then this could be a song composed for Solomon's wedding to some foreign princess. As such it has points of contact with Psalm 45, a psalm celebrating a royal wedding, although it makes no specific mention of Solomon.

If it is not a song composed for Solomon's wedding and preserved in an anthology, how does it fit in with the rest of the book? Those who read the book as a drama have seen in this section the account of Solomon's seizure and seduction of a country girl. Others have regarded it as an act in a cultic drama with the king playing the role of the god of fertility. The view taken here is that this passage has nothing to do with Solomon's wedding. The lovers are looking forward to the day of their own wedding.

For a young couple being married in a small country church today, that day is for them just as much a right royal day as the most splendid royal wedding celebrated in Westminster Abbey or St Paul's. There is indeed evidence from rabbinic sources which suggest that before the days of sorrow for the Jewish people, which began with the destruction of Jerusalem and the Temple by the Romans in A.D. 70, the bride and groom both wore crowns at Jewish weddings. This was their royal day.

It is likely that throughout this passage we are again listening to the girl giving voice to her thoughts. She begins in verse 6 briefly describing herself, coming prepared for her great day. She then (v. 7) thinks of her lover, in her eyes every inch a king. She thinks of him as King Solomon, escorted by a royal bodyguard, coming to his wedding on a richly decorated sedan chair. This is the "day of the gladness of his heart" (v. 11); so their own wedding day will be just such a day of joy and gladness.

Let us look at the passage in a little more detail. Here comes the bride (v. 6), "coming up from the wilderness". Because of its geographical location you always 'come up' to Jerusalem in the Old Testament, and it is in Jerusalem that any royal wedding would be celebrated. So she comes up from "the wilderness", which may mean no more than from the country. The word translated wilderness (GNB "desert") does not mean what we tend to mean by a desert. Rather it indicates any region of rough natural pasturage lacking any permanent human settlement. Although the "column [literally "pillars"] of smoke" may refer merely to the dust raised by the wedding procession as it moves across the dry land, it could also be a description of the fragrant incense which accompanies her, with myrrh (see 1:13) and frankincense, another gum resin covered with whitish dust which is one of the ingredients used in the preparation of incense (Exod. 30:34). Myrrh and frankincense appear again in the man's description of the seductive fragrance of his beloved in 4:6. They were among the gifts brought to Jesus by the wise men according to Matthew 2:11.

Here comes the groom (vv. 7–11). The royal bridegroom comes in his "litter", a word which elsewhere in the Old Testament means a bed or a couch. The picture is probably that of a portable divan. It may mean the same as his "palanquin" or sedan chair referred to in verse 9. He comes escorted by "sixty mighty men"—"soldiers" or "warriors" (GNB, NEB)—his hand-picked, personal entourage (cf. the list of David's "mighty men" in 2 Sam. 23:8–39). They are ready to defend him against "alarms at night" (v. 8). This phrase is perhaps best taken to refer to the unexpected night attacks that bandits were always liable to make upon a rich caravanserie. The New English Bible's translation, "the demon of the night" (v. 8), assumes a reference to dangerous spirits that were often thought to attack the bride and the groom on their wedding night. Remember the sad tale in the Apocrypha of Sarah who had seven husbands killed on their wedding night by the evil demon Asmodeus, before Tobias came to the rescue (Tobit 3:7ff.). While Tobias may have smoked out the demon by his foul-smelling concoction (Tobit 6:15ff.), it is hard to see how the swords of the warriors could be of much help in this situation!

Some of the detail in the description of the royal palanquin in verses 9–10 is far from clear. The "silver posts" probably held up the protecting canopy; its "back"—the word occurs only here in the Old Testament—could be either its upholstery or the canopy stretched over the top. The phrase which the RSV translates "it was lovingly wrought within" has been interpreted in many different ways. The New English Bible's, "and its lining was of leather", interprets the word normally translated "love" in the light of a similar Arabic word meaning leather. There have been many other guesses, both as to the meaning of this word and as to how it should be linked with the following words. On the whole it seems best to think of the interior of this royal palanquin as decorated with tapestries depicting love scenes. The poem concludes with an invitation to the "daughters of Jerusalem" or "the daughters of Zion"—Zion being strictly the Temple site in Jerusalem—to come out and greet the king on his joyful wedding day. The mention of the king's mother placing a crown or wreath upon his head recalls the prominent role that Solomon's mother Bathsheba played in his accession to the throne and in the early years of his reign.

Is there an ironic undertone to this comparison of the lover to Solomon, as this young couple look forward to their own royal day? Solomon, you remember, had "seven hundred wives, princesses and three hundred concubines" (1 Kings 11:3). They did something to his "heart"; they turned it away from the God who is the source of all true joy. This young couple pledge themselves totally and exclusively to each other, on a day which is to be "the day of the gladness of his heart" (v. 11). There is a joy to be discovered in such an exclusive relationship which cannot be experienced by those who believe that in this, as in all other things in life, variety is the spice of life.

PERFECTION

Song of Solomon 4:1-7

[1]Behold, you are beautiful, my love,
  behold, you are beautiful!
Your eyes are doves
  behind your veil.
Your hair is like a flock of goats,
  moving down the slopes of Gilead.
[2]Your teeth are like a flock of shorn ewes
  that have come up from the washing,
all of which bear twins,
  and not one among them is bereaved.
[3]Your lips are like a scarlet thread,
  and your mouth is lovely.
Your cheeks are like halves of a pomegranate
  behind your veil.
[4]Your neck is like the tower of David,
  built for an arsenal,
whereon hang a thousand bucklers,
  all of them shields of warriors.
[5]Your two breasts are like two fawns,
  twins of a gazelle,
    that feed among the lillies.

⁶Until the day breathes
    and the shadows flee,
 I will hie me to the mountain of myrrh
    and the hill of frankincense.
⁷You are all fair, my love;
    there is no flaw in you.

This is the first example in the book of what is, in Arabic, known technically as a *wasf*, a poem which dwells upon and praises the physical beauty of the beloved. In the first five verses the man describes the beauty of his beloved from her eyes down to her breasts. It is a carefully crafted poem with the opening words of the last verse (v. 7) echoing the words of the first verse. It is difficult to see why the RSV translated "you are beautiful, my love" in verse 1, but "you are all fair, my love" in verse 7, since the same Hebrew word lies behind beautiful and fair (see comment on 1:8). One by one he notes the physical charms of the lady in his life. The opening description, "Your eyes are doves", echoes 1:15 (see comment there for the comparison of eyes to doves), adding "behind your veil". It may be the timidity of the dove sheltering in the crannies in the cliff, needing to be coaxed out, which is in the poet's mind. So the eyes are there "hiding" behind the veil; yet the veil, which is intended to discourage unauthorized glances, has in some ways the opposite effect, making the eyes mysteriously more attractive and enticing.

Your eyes . . . your hair: the comparison of the hair to "a flock of goats, moving down the slopes of Gilead", may seem somewhat bizarre to us. It is probably intended to convey two ideas. Goats were black, so was her hair (see comment on 1:5); goats streamed down the slopes of the hillside, so this suggests the flowing, lively movement of her long hair. The mountains of Gilead formed a high plateau towering over the Jordan valley on its eastern side opposite the mountains of Samaria and South Galilee.

Your eyes . . . your hair . . . your teeth: they are compared to a well tended flock of sheep, dipped and sheared, hence white. The reference to all of them bearing twins has caused difficulty, since there is evidence that ewes bearing twins were not common in the ancient world. This, however, may be the point; her teeth, upper and lower are, like twins, perfectly matched with no unsightly gaps between, and in this she is unusual. The lady would obviously be a perfect advert for any of the popular brand names of toothpaste.

Your eyes . . . your hair . . . your teeth . . . your lips: they are a vivid red, like the lips of well groomed Egyptian ladies who went in for a form of lipstick. They are lovely lips from which come charming words (cf. NEB, the Hebrew which the RSV translates "your mouth" in v. 3 is literally "your words").

Your eyes . . . your hair . . . your teeth . . . your lips . . . your cheeks: the word rendered "cheeks" occurs only here, in a parallel passage in 6:7 and in the story of Jael the wife of Heber the Kenite who hammers a tent peg through the "temples" of Sisera the exhausted Canaanite commander in Judges 4:21; 5:26. Hence the variety of translations suggested: New English Bible "parted lips", New International Version "temples". Cheeks, however, make perfectly good sense here. The bright red seeds of the pomegranate with the touch of white covering in the membrane which separates the seeds, provides a neat picture of the attractively coloured cheeks glowing through the veil.

Your eyes . . . your hair . . . your teeth . . . your lips . . . your cheeks . . . your neck: It is doubtful whether many of today's beauties would be flattered by having their necks compared to a "tower". What "the tower of David" was we do not know. There may be a reference to it in Nehemiah 3:25 where among the sections of the wall of the city being repaired there is mention of the part opposite "the tower projecting from the upper house of the king at the court of the guard". But what is the picture intended in the rest of verse 4? Instead of translating "built for an arsenal" or "round and smooth" (GNB), we should probably follow the New English Bible with its description of the tower "built with winding courses". As we know, particularly from Egyptian scenes, women often wore a deep necklace made up of row upon row of beads. These rows of beads are likened to the courses of stones that went into the building of the tower, and the individual and often differently coloured beads which make up the rows are compared to warrior's shields or weapons hanging on the wall of the tower, glinting in the sun, giving it colour and added attractiveness.

Lastly, "your two breasts": small, firm breasts were regarded as a sign of beauty. Using a delicate nature image of two fawns grazing, the grace and beauty of two well formed breasts are indicated.

Verse 6 is a deliberate echo of 2:17 (see comment there) where the girl tells her lover that he must depart as day breaks. Yes, I will go, says her lover, but not to any distant mountains, only as far as the "mountain of myrrh" and "the hill of frankincense", almost certainly a reference to her fragrant breasts. It is almost as if he says, 'I will fall anywhere you like, provided it is into your arms'. There are no snide innuendos at this point, no crudity, only a frank acknowledgment of and delight in the physical charms of the beloved. To try, as some have done, to spiritualize this poem by giving an allegorical meaning to the different parts of the body, is not only to destroy the poem, but implicitly to deny that sexuality and the delight that man and woman have in each other is one of the good gifts of the creator God to whom the Bible as a whole bears witness.

LOVE'S FULFILMENT

Song of Solomon 4:8–5:1

8Come with me from Lebanon, my bride;
    come with me from Lebanon.
  Depart from the peak of Amana,
    from the peak of Senir and Hermon,
  from the dens of lions,
    from the mountains of leopards.
9You have ravished my heart, my sister, my bride,
    you have ravished my heart with a glance of your eyes,
    with one jewel of your necklace.
10How sweet is your love, my sister, my bride!
    how much better is your love than wine,
    and the fragrance of your oils than any spice!

¹¹Your lips distil nectar, my bride;
  honey and milk are under your tongue;
  the scent of your garments is like the scent of Lebanon.
¹²A garden locked is my sister, my bride,
  a garden locked, a fountain sealed.
¹³Your shoots are an orchard of pomegranates
  with all choicest fruits,
  henna with nard,
¹⁴nard and saffron, calamus and cinnamon,
  with all trees of frankincense,
 myrrh and aloes,
  with all chief spices—
¹⁵a garden fountain, a well of living water
  and flowing streams from Lebanon.

¹⁶Awake, O north wind,
  and come, O south wind!
 Blow upon my garden,
  let its fragrance be wafted abroad.
 Let my beloved come to his garden,
  and eat its choicest fruits.

¹I come to my garden, my sister, my bride,
  I gather my myrrh with my spice,
  I eat my honeycomb with my honey,
  I drink my wine with my milk.

 Eat, O friends, and drink:
  drink deeply, O lovers!

The pace quickens. The eagerness of the lovers and the fulfilment they find or hope to find in each other, are now depicted. We begin in verse 8 with the lover who has just been extolling the beauty of his beloved, issuing an invitation. Most modern translations follow the Greek text at the beginning of the verse and read "Come", instead of the Hebrew, which has a second "with me". This is hardly necessary. The two-fold occurrence of "with me" is emphatic, "with me . . . with me you shall come [or travel]". But what does it mean to come *from* Lebanon and *from* the hills of Lebanon? Why is the girl away up there in the far north? It makes much more sense, and is grammatically possible, to translate not *from* Lebanon, but *to* Lebanon. The invitation the lover extends to her is to go away with him far from the madding crowd. Up

north there is some distant, remote spot where they may be alone
with their love. It is as if he is saying to her, 'Come, let us go and
find our own Shangri-la'. Amana (v. 8) is not otherwise known as
the name of a mountain in the Old Testament, but it is probably
the mountain which is the source of the river Amana or Abana
(see 2 Kings 5:12) which flows through Damascus. It is today the
river Barada. Senir and Hermon seem to be variant names (Deut.
3:9) for the highest of the Lebanese mountains, over 9000 feet in
height. From its foothills flows the river Jordan. The reference to
these hills being the haunt of lions and leopards (or panthers)
serves to underline their remoteness. Both lions and leopards
were familiar in ancient Israel (see Hos. 13:7).

The invitation is issued to "my bride", a word that occurs in
every verse of this passage from verse 8 to 12 and also in 5:1. On
four occasions it is joined with the word sister, "my sister, my
bride". Both words, "bride" and "sister", are found frequently as
terms of affection and endearment in ancient love poetry; the
word "bride" no more implies that the wedding has taken place
than the word "sister" points to some incestuous relationship. As
used by the lover in this poem the term "bride" may indeed be
looking forward to the day when their love will be consummated
in marriage, but it does not turn this poem, as some have argued,
into a wedding song.

The powerful sexual attraction that the girl has for her lover is
spelled out in verses 9–11. The Hebrew words translated "you
have ravished my heart", which occur twice in verse 9 could
equally well be translated 'you have inflamed me' or 'you have
aroused my passion'. Just a glance from her eyes, or the sight of
one strand in her necklace, and he is under her spell. This he
expresses in verse 10 by echoing words that she has earlier used of
him in 1:2–3 (see comment there). The picture of her lips dropping nectar or liquid honey, and of milk and honey under her
tongue, conveys the delectable sweetness of her kisses (cf. Prov.
5:3). The scent of Lebanon is the scent of the cedar forests of
Lebanon, distinctive, overpowering, as is "the scent of your
garments" (v. 11). We may compare Psalm 45 where the royal
bride's dresses are said to be "fragrant with myrrh and aloes and

cassia' (Ps. 45:8). The word translated "garment" here, however, is the word that usually denotes the large outer wrap which is used as a coat by day and a blanket by night. It was on such a garment that the proofs of virginity were supposed to be produced as evidence on the wedding night (see Deut. 22:17–18). There is therefore probably a sexual overtone to the use of this word here. We may get near the sense implicit in it if we translate it as négligé or night dress.

Utterly desirable, but as yet unattainable—this is what is implied in the description of the beloved in verse 12 as "a garden locked" and "a fountain [or spring] sealed". The garden image, like that of the vineyard in 2:15, is used here for the girl and her sexuality. It is an image which we can trace in the love poetry of ancient Egypt and Mesopotamia, as well as in ancient Greece. It is an image that poets have continued to use across the centuries; compare Tennyson's description: "One rose of the rosebud garden of girls". The girl is described as "a locked garden", to stress her modesty, her sexual exclusiveness, perhaps her virginity. But it may also point to her lover's longing to enter this locked garden; similarly with "the fountain sealed" or "the sealed spring". In its injunction to marital fidelity, Proverbs 5:15–18 describes the wife as a cistern or fountain and warns the man that he should not allow her springs to overflow into the road: "let them be yours alone, not shared with strangers" (NEB). Here it is a sealed spring from which the lover longs to drink and refresh himself.

The tantalizing delights of the locked garden are then evoked. It is an orchard—the Hebrew here uses the Persian loan word *pardes* from which comes our word paradise (cf. Eccles. 2:5). It is an orchard well watered by 'irrigation channels' (v. 13), which gives better sense than RSV's "shoots" or New English Bible's "cheeks". In it grow pomegranates and all kinds of delectable fruits. It is a garden which produces all kinds of perfumes and spices, some of which have featured already in the poems: nard, henna, myrrh (1:12–13), frankincense (3:6). Saffron (v.14) is mentioned only here in the Old Testament: it is a scented powder produced from the dried, crushed stigmas of the saffron crocus:

calamus or "sweet cane" (NEB) is a type of wild grass which gives off a gingery smell; cinnamon comes from the bark of a tree and was used as an ingredient in the sacred consecrating oil (Exod. 30:23); aloes was an aromatic resin derived from a tree native to India. All these perfumes or spices have links in one way or another with sexual attractiveness. As one commentator has put it, 'this is a groovy grove', an orchard filled with fruits and plants evocative of love. It has its own "garden fountain" (v. 15), a fountain of clear running water that comes, as it were, cascading down from its source in the Lebanon hills.

Unattainable? No, says the girl in reply (v. 16). She summons the winds to carry fragrance from her garden to her lover. She invites him to enter the garden and taste its choicest fruits. She is his to have completely and unreservedly. Quickly he responds (5:1). Before many of the words which have already appeared in previous verses, he adds the all important little word "my": my garden . . . my myrrh . . . my spice . . . my honeycomb . . . my honey . . . my wine . . . my milk—mine and mine alone to enjoy.

The last two lines of 5:1 are probably a comment by the daughters of Jerusalem encouraging the lovers to have their fill of the love which unites them. Eating and drinking is an oft repeated metaphor for making love. We could imagine these lovers singing to each other:

Drink to me only with thine eyes,
    And I will pledge with mine.
Or leave a kiss within the cup,
    And I'll not look for wine.
The thirst that from the soul doth rise
    Doth ask a drink divine;
But might I of Jove's nectar sup,
    I would not change for thine.   (Ben Jonson)

A DISTURBING DREAM

Song of Solomon 5:2–8

²I slept, but my heart was awake.
Hark! my beloved is knocking.

"Open to me, my sister, my love,
　　my dove my perfect one;
for my head is wet with dew,
　　my locks with the drops of the night."
³I had put off my garment,
　　how could I put it on?
　I had bathed my feet,
　　how could I soil them?
⁴My beloved put his hands to the latch,
　　and my heart was thrilled within me.
⁵I arose to open to my beloved,
　　and my hands dripped with myrrh,
　my fingers with liquid myrrh,
　　upon the handles of the bolt.
⁶I opened to my beloved,
　　but my beloved had turned and gone.
　My soul failed me when he spoke.
　I sought him, but found him not;
　　I called him, but he gave no answer.
⁷The watchmen found me,
　　as they went about in the city;
　they beat me, they wounded me,
　　they took away my mantle,
　　those watchmen of the walls.
⁸I adjure you, O daughters of Jerusalem,
　　if you find my beloved,
　that you tell him
　　I am sick with love.

Chapter 5:2 to chapter 6:3 is best taken as one long poem. It is
only for the sake of convenience that we break it after 5:8. The
meaning we give to the next section, 5:9ff., depends entirely on
our approach to 5:2–8. There have been many ways of interpreting this poem. It has been taken to be the description of a lovers'
tryst, which because of a misunderstanding proved abortive. It
has been regarded as a break in the lovers' relationship, one of the
'downs' in the ups and downs of love's experience, and thus a
realistic handling of the difficulties that can arise in even the best
of human relationships. The view taken here is that like 3:1–5 it is

a dream, a dream which mirrors the joys and the anxieties in the girl's mind.

There are close similarities with earlier parts of the book. As in 2:8ff. she imagines her lover coming to her, standing outside her house. As in 3:1–5 she is in bed. She gets up and sets out on what initially proves to be a vain search for her lover. In the course of it she has an encounter with the night watchmen in the city. But there are differences. In 2:17 she tells her lover to depart as dawn breaks: here, after what looks like a piece of female coquetry, she goes to the door to find to her disappointment that he has gone. In 3:3 the night watchmen treat her with apparent indifference: here they lay hands on her and take her for a streetwalker. Why else, after all, would a scantily clothed girl be wandering the streets at night? Perhaps in this dream she is more conscious of the fact that her attitude to her lover, and her actions, are liable to be misunderstood by society.

In her dream she imagines herself sleeping somewhat fitfully and restlessly—"my heart [or mind] was awake" (v. 2), her mind too full of thoughts of her lover to allow her to sink into the peaceful oblivion of sleep. Suddenly she hears her lover "knocking". The same Hebrew word is used in Judges 19:22 of a crowd of men hammering at the door of a house to gain entrance. Presumably here it indicates a gentle tap, either at the door or at the lattice window, otherwise the whole household would have been wakened, thus defeating the purpose of a midnight assignation. With gentle words of endearment, "my sister, my love, my dove, my perfect [or flawless] one", he seeks admittance out of the damp coldness of the night air.

She begins to tease him (v. 3), perhaps to mask her own subconscious hesitations. I am in bed, why should I get dressed again to come to open the door? My feet have been washed, why should I get them dirty again walking across the floor? It is as if she is teasingly challenging him. Tell me, why should I put myself out to let you in? He becomes impatient (v. 4). He puts his hand to the latch, literally 'from [or on] the hole'. It could be that he puts his hand through the lattice window hoping to find her reaching out to grasp it, or he puts his hand through the latch hole, hoping to be able to open the door from the inside. Either way he is disappointed: she is playing difficult to get. Emotionally, however, she is quivering with excitement: "my heart was thrilled within me" (v. 4) or as the New English Bible more literally renders, "my bowels stirred within me", not the most felicitous of phrases for modern ears. The bowels are, however, in Hebrew, thought to be the seat of intense emotions (see Jer. 4:19, AV, NEB). They are also associated with procreation. If we translate as the Jerusalem Bible does, "I trembled to the core to my being", then that trembling or thrill has a strongly sexual element in it. By the time she gets up, heavily perfumed—she had probably been expecting her lover—and reaches the door, he is gone (v.5). She has overplayed her hand. She is left standing, disappointed. "My soul failed me when he spoke" (v. 6) is not a very happy rendering of a phrase which could mean either "I wanted to hear his voice" (GNB) or even "I nearly died when I found he had gone".

Out into the night she goes vainly seeking him, only to be roughly handled by the watchmen (v. 7). She turns to her companions, the daughters of Jerusalem (v. 8) as she has done before (2:7, 3:5), to make them promise—promise what? The Good News Bible's, "you will tell him I am weak with passion", suggests that she wishes them to inform her lover that in spite of what has happened she is still incurably in love with him. On the other hand, the statement could be taken to mean that she does not want them to tell her lover something; that something being that she is sick or tired of making love to him. Of course she is not.

Her dream makes perfectly good sense interpreted in this way, but there may be another level of meaning similar to the double meaning we have already traced in the words "garden" and "vineyard". In several passages from literature outside the Old Testament and within the Old Testament (*eg* Isa. 57:8, RSV "nakedness"; 2 Sam. 11:8), the words "hand" and "feet" are used as euphemisms for the sexual organs. Likewise the word translated "latch" or "hole" could have similar connotations: "my beloved put his hand to the latch" in verse 4 could therefore be a description of sexual intercourse. The verb "open" which occurs in verses 2, 5 and 6, in each case without an object, may be similarly interpreted. In this case we are dealing with a woman who has been sexually aroused and is desperately longing for further gratification of her sexual desires. It is strange how certain older commentators, aware of this meaning, tended to dismiss it as 'obscene'. This is to read our perverted sense of values into the biblical text, instead of allowing the text to speak to us frankly of sexuality as one of God's good gifts to man and woman.

QUESTION AND ANSWER

Song of Solomon 5:9–6:3

> [9]What is your beloved more than another beloved,
>   O fairest among women?
> What is your beloved more than another beloved,
>   that you thus adjure us?
>
> [10]My beloved is all radiant and ruddy,
>   distinguished among ten thousand.
> [11]His head is the finest gold;
>   his locks are wavy,
>   black as a raven.
> [12]His eyes are like doves
>   beside springs of water,
> bathed in milk,
>   fitly set.
> [13]His cheeks are like beds of spices,
>   yielding fragrance.
> His lips are lilies,
>   distilling liquid myrrh.
> [14]His arms are rounded gold,
>   set with jewels.
> His body is ivory work,
>   encrusted with sapphires.
> [15]His legs are alabaster columns,
>   set upon bases of gold.
> His appearance is like Lebanon,
>   choice as the cedars.

¹⁶His speech is most sweet,
  and he is altogether desirable.
This is my beloved and this is my friend,
  O daughters of Jerusalem.

¹Whither has your beloved gone,
  O fairest among women?
Whither has your beloved turned,
  that we may seek him with you?

²My beloved has gone down to his garden,
  to the beds of spices,
to pasture his flock in the gardens,
  and to gather lilies.
³I am my beloved's and my beloved is mine;
  he pastures his flock among the lilies.

In her dream, the girl's companions immediately respond to the promise she asks them to make by mockingly echoing the words her lover had used to describe her: "O fairest among women" (see 1:8). They then inquire, 'What's so special about this lover of yours?' (v. 9).

She replies in verses 10–16 in one of the few poems which have come down to us from the ancient world in which a girl describes the physical charms of her lover. This is the parallel to his praise of her beauty which we find in 4:1–7 and again in 7:1–9. She dwells upon the colour, shape, strength and beauty of his body from his head down to his legs or thighs. She begins with a general comment in verse 10. He stands out from other men because he glows with health. He is "radiant" (this Hebrew word usually describes something bright or shiny): he is "ruddy" (this word has the idea of redness in it and probably indicates a deep, healthy tan). It is used in the description of David when he is first introduced to Samuel: "he was ruddy and had beautiful eyes, and was handsome" (1 Sam. 16:12), all attributes that this girl sees in her lover.

His head ... "the finest gold", a phrase which joins together two different Hebrew words for gold to heighten the effect. The Good News Bible's "bronzed and smooth" is probably too pedestrian. This is the exaggerated language of a girl in love.

His head . . . his locks: "wavy" (NEB, "like palm fronds"), long flowing hair is probably intended; "black as a raven", black hair being the sign of someone in the prime of life (see comment on Eccles. 11:10).

His head . . . his locks . . . his eyes: here she returns his compliment, "like doves" (see 1:15). It is not wholly clear what is meant by this comparison or how we are to take the words which follow. The words the RSV translates "fitly set", presumably giving the idea of eyes set in the face like sparkling jewels, could equally well be rendered 'sitting by a brimming pool'. Although there is no evidence elsewhere for doves bathing in milk, it may be that the picture of doves perched beside a clear pool or swimming in milk, is intended to convey the attractiveness of the dark iris of the eye surrounded by the clear whiteness of the rest of the eye.

His head . . . his locks . . . his eyes . . . . his cheeks: the Hebrew has "beds of spices and towers of perfumes"; the latter phrase the New English Bible interprets as "chests full of perfumes" (v. 13). A simple alteration to the Hebrew text lies behind the RSV, "yielding [or exuding] fragrance". He probably made liberal use of the oil of Turaq (see comment on 1:3). After his cheeks come his lips, the source of the most delectable and sweet kisses (cf. 4:11). From the head and its attractive qualities, she moves down to the rest of his body. His arms (literally his hands) are like "rounded gold". The word translated "rounded" is used normally to describe some kind of round bar. The New English Bible retains something of the flavour of this when it renders, "his hands are golden rods set in topaz". The Hebrew word *tarshish,* translated by RSV "jewels", can either be one of several place names, ranging from the Mediterranean to India, or the name of a precious stone whose identity is doubtful; compare the way in which we talk about a "Cairngorm" stone. It is debatable whether again we should regard this as the exaggerated language of a lover or whether we should render it rather more prosaically as the Good News Bible does: "His hands are well formed, and he wears rings set with gems" (v. 14).

His arms or hands . . . his body: what the second half of verse 14 is intended to convey is very uncertain. Perhaps the attractive whiteness of an ivory panel is being used to convey the smooth flatness of his muscular stomach, but it is anyone's guess what "encrusted with sapphires" or "overlaid with lapis lazuli" (NEB) means.

His arms or hands...his body...his legs: the strength and beauty of his legs or thighs is indicated by comparing them to "alabaster columns, set upon bases of gold". The book of Ecclesiasticus (26:18) uses similar language to describe a woman's shapely legs: "Like a golden pillar on a silver base, is a shapely leg with a firm foot".

Nothing is too costly or exotic that it cannot be used to describe this incomparable lover of hers.

Grant her a poet's licence. It is no greater than the licence Francis Thompson uses to describe a snowflake:

> What heart could have thought of you?
>   Fashioned so purely,
>   Fragilely, surely,
>   From what paradisal,
>   Imaginative metal,
>   Too costly for cost?

Tall, strong, handsome as the cedars of Lebanon, wholly desirable, mine—that is what my beloved, my darling, is like, she says to the daughters of Jerusalem: there is the answer to your question (v. 16).

Her companions seem convinced. Their sole desire now is to help her to find her lover (6:1); how can they help? The girl's reply in 6:2–3 implies that she does not need their help to find him. She knows where he is (for the language of 6:2–3, see 2:16; 4:12); her fears have been groundless. He has not left her. Some commentators have been worried by the girl's reply. Why did she ask her companions to help her to find her lover if she knew where he was all the time? But this is not the cold logic of everyday life. It is the logic of a lover's dream. The dream that began with her troubled thoughts in 5:2 has found its happy ending. She is sure of her lover. Just as earlier she had described their relationship in the words, "My beloved is mine and I am his" (2:16), so now she plays a variation on the same theme, reversing the order, "I am my beloved's and my beloved is mine" (6:3). In her dreams she had set out to discover her lost lover: she found 'journey's end in lover's meeting'.

THE LOVER'S RESPONSE

Song of Solomon 6:4–12

> 4You are beautiful as Tirzah, my love,
>   comely as Jerusalem,
>   terrible as an army with banners.
> 5Turn away your eyes from me,
>   for they disturb me—
> Your hair is like a flock of goats,
>   moving down the slopes of Gilead.
> 6Your teeth are like a flock of ewes,
>   that have come up from the washing,
> all of them bear twins,
>   not one among them is bereaved.
> 7Your cheeks are like halves of a pomegranate
>   behind your veil.
> 8There are sixty queens and eighty concubines,
>   and maidens without number.
> 9My dove, my perfect one, is only one,
>   the darling of her mother,
>   flawless to her that bore her.
> The maidens saw her and called her happy;
>   the queens and concubines also,
>   and they praised her.
> 10"Who is this that looks forth like the dawn,
>   fair as the moon, bright as the sun,
>   terrible as an army with banners?"
> 11I went down to the nut orchard,
>   to look at the blossoms of the valley,
> to see whether the vines had budded,
>   whether the pomegranates were in bloom.
> 12Before I was aware, my fancy set me
>   in a chariot beside my prince.

The girl's dream has climaxed in a declaration of the unbreakable relationship which unites her with her lover. Her lover now responds, first by returning to the theme of the incomparable beauty of his beloved (vv. 4–10), and then by acknowledging the power she has over him, the way in which she turns him on (vv. 11–12).

With minor variations, verses 5*b*–7 are a repetition of 4:1*b*–3. The language of love bears repeating. It is but the outward expression of a lasting relationship. The passage also begins by echoing the opening words of chapter 4, "You are beautiful, my love", but then it proceeds to use two new pictures to describe her beauty—the one in verse 4, the other in verse 10. Each picture is capped by the same phrase which, as you can see from English translations, has been variously understood. The RSV has "terrible as an army with banners" in both places; the Good News Bible offers two different translations, adding in each case "Hebrew unclear", the New English Bible omits the phrase in verse 4 and translates in verse 10, "majestic as the starry heavens". Perhaps it is best to take the phrase to mean on each occasion, 'awesome to look at', with the proviso that 'awesome' when applied to the girl's beauty may mean little more than our expression 'You look terrific'.

In verse 4 her beauty is compared to that of Tirzah and Jerusalem. Tirzah, probably modern Tell el-Farah some seven miles north-east of Nablus (ancient Shechem), was the first capital of the northern kingdom of Israel after the split up of Solomon's kingdom. It was replaced as capital by Samaria during the reign of Omri (1 Kings 16:23–34). A former royal residence, a present royal residence, the once capital of the north, the continuing capital of the south—Tirzah and Jerusalem—what more appropriate images of one who was enthroned in this young man's thoughts! We could substitute place names like Perth and London, or Richmond and Washington. From such earth-bound places of beauty the lover turns in verse 10 to compare his beloved to the rising dawn, to the glory of the moon, to the brightness of the sun. The wonder and beauty in the heavens above have been a recurring theme in the language of love in all ages; see Shake-speare's *Romeo and Juliet* for example:

> But, soft! what light through yonder window breaks?
> It is the east, and Juliet is the sun.

Previously in the poem, so much of which he repeats here, the lover has drawn attention to the attractiveness of his beloved's eyes, comparing them for example to "doves" (4:1; cf. 1:15). But, as he now admits in the first part of verse 5, they have a disturbing attractiveness. He can hardly bear to look into her eyes. Turn them away, he says, "for they disturb me", they bowl me over, they excite me. This is better than the New English Bible's "they dazzle me". Yet if her beauty is disturbing, it is also (moving to v. 8) incomparable. Sixty princesses . . . eighty concubines . . . other young women without number—you can have the lot, he says. Sixty . . . eighty . . . without number, is a Hebrew way of using ascending numbers to indicate an indefinite number (see Amos 1:3). Women you may have, he says, as many as you like, from any social class you like, but for me there is only one woman in my life, one woman, "my dove, my perfect one" (see v. 9; 5:2); one woman whose fine qualities have been recognized from her birth, since she was her mother's favourite child. The New English Bible's translation in verse 9, "devoted to the mother who bore her", gets the wrong end of the stick. It is not the girl's attitude to her mother that is being noted, but the fact that she was the apple of her mother's eye. With that conceit born of love he depicts all other women coming to congratulate her and to praise her beauty.

The last two verses in this section, verses 11–12, pick up the thought that has already been expressed in verse 5; that here is beauty which disturbs and excites a lover. He imagines himself coming to his garden of love (see 5:1). It is spring time, the time of awakening life. He is there under the nut or walnut trees. Again there is some evidence for the walnut having erotic associations. The young plants, the greenery (hardly "the rushes", NEB) is beginning to carpet the valley; the fruit trees show signs of life. The lover is . . . what?

The last verse, verse 12, is generally considered to be the most difficult verse in the book. A glance at modern translations will show the variety of approaches to the problem it poses:

RSV—Before I was aware, my fancy set me
          in a chariot beside my prince.
GNB—I am trembling; you have made me
          as eager for love
          as a chariot driver is for battle.
NEB—I did not know myself;
          she made me feel more than a prince
          reigning over the myriads of his people.

All indicate their hesitations about the translations they offer, and such hesitations have been there from the earliest times. If the RSV, or something similar is correct—and this seems unlikely—verses 11–12 must be put onto the lips of the woman. Other translations, probably correctly, try to convey to us the high state of excitement, the sexual desire which now grips the man.

THE DANCE OF LOVE

Song of Solomon 6:13–7:9

13Return, return, O Shulammite,
          return, return, that we may look upon you.

Why should you look upon the Shulammite,
          as upon a dance before two armies?
1How graceful are your feet in sandals,
          O queenly maiden!
Your rounded thighs are like jewels,
          the work of a master hand.
2Your naval is a rounded bowl
          that never lacks mixed wine.
Your belly is a heap of wheat,
          encircled with lilies.
3Your two breasts are like two fawns,
          twins of a gazelle.

⁴Your neck is like an ivory tower.
  Your eyes are like pools in Heshbon,
    by the gate of Bath-rabbim.
  Your nose is like a tower of Lebanon,
    overlooking Damascus.
⁵Your head crowns you like Carmel,
    and your flowing locks are like purple;
    a king is held captive in the tresses.

⁶How fair and pleasant you are,
    O loved one, delectable maiden!
⁷You are stately as a palm tree,
    and your breasts are like its clusters.
⁸I say I will climb the palm tree
    and lay hold of its branches.
  Oh, may your breasts be like clusters of the vine,
    and the scent of your breath like apples,
⁹and your kisses like the best wine
    that goes down smoothly,
    gliding over lips and teeth.

This section has its own difficult questions of interpretation. Who is speaking? How many different speakers are there? How are we to divide the verses between different speakers? The view taken here is as follows:

  6:13*a* is an invitation addressed to the woman by her companions;
  6:13*b* is her modest or coy response;
  7:1–5 contain the reassuring comments of her companions about her physical charms;
  7:6–9*a* reveal her lover joining in to dwell in a much more personal and intimate way on the delights which her love has to offer.

(a) Verse 13*a*: Four times we hear the echoing word "return" (Hebrew *shuv*). Such repetition is common in Hebrew poetry in eager or urgent requests; compare the opening words of Isaiah chapter 40, "Comfort, comfort...". But return from where? The assumption seems to be that she has been separated temporarily from her companions and her lover. They are now inviting her to come back quickly. The Good News Bible's translation, "Dance, dance...", assumes a slight alteration to the vowels in the Hebrew text to give the meaning "leap". In this case the call is not to return, but to begin to dance, probably a dance associated with wedding festivities, and a dance which will display her physical charms to perfection. Although most of our English translations address the girl as the "Shulammite" or "girl of Shulam" (GNB), this translation is by no means certain. It is the only time this word occurs in the Old Testament; and it is assumed that by the time the poem was written the town otherwise known to us in the Old Testament as Shunem in the valley of Esdraelon, was already being called Shulam, as it is in later documents. It would also be possible to give the word different vowels and to take it to mean "Solomon's girl" or "perfect one" (a different adjective from that in 6:9).

(b) Verse 13*b*: The girl coyly asks why people should want to see her perform "a dance before two armies". Both the New English Bible and the Good News Bible assume, probably correctly, that the "armies" or camps are lines of dancers (NEB) or onlookers (GNB) present at the festivities. Although the word translated "armies" can also be the place name Mahanaim (RSV ftn.), there is no evidence for a 'dance of Mahanaim' being the name of a well known dance in the same way as we talk of a Strathspey. It is almost as if she is saying, 'Why, when there are so many present willing to join in a military two-step, why ask for a solo performance from me?'

(c) 7:1–5: Dance, however, she does, much to the delight of the onlookers who praise the physical charms, from sandalled feet to dark flowing tresses, of this "queenly maiden", a term of endearment (see comment on 1:4), hence the justification for the Good News Bible's "What a wonderful girl you are!". It is evident from the description which follows that she dances virtually naked or clothed only in diaphanous veils which serve only to accentuate her physical attractiveness. As she sways in the dance, the 'curves' of her thighs seem like jewels or ornaments shaped to perfection by the hands of a skilled craftsman. Her "navel"—the only other clear use of this word in the Old Testament is in Ezekiel 16:4 where it refers to the umbilical cord—is compared to "a rounded bowl". Such bowls were usually large, but it is not the size, but rather the perfectly formed shape of the navel, which

seems to be in mind. Although most translations take the second
line in verse 2 to be a description of the bowl "that never lacks
mixed [or spiced] wine", it could equally be taken as a wish, "May
it never lack spiced wine". A bowl filled with spiced wine is
attractive and stimulating, so the hope is being expressed that her
navel will never lose its power to stimulate and attract. The
comparison of her belly to "a heap of wheat" probably highlights
its gentle symmetrical curves or its rich tawny colour. Such heaps
of wheat were sometimes hedged around with thorns to prevent
the wheat being scattered and to keep off animals; but this
"heap" is encircled not with thorns but with lilies (see comment
on 2:1–2). Her breasts are described as in 4:5 (see comment
there). Her neck which in 4:4 was likened to the tower of David,
is here likened to an "ivory tower" which may draw attention to
its pale colour or to the ivory necklaces which adorn it. Her eyes,
previously compared to doves (1:15; 4:1) are described as "pools
in Heshbon". These pools are not running springs, but reservoirs
for storing water. Remains of such reservoirs have been exca-
vated at the site of ancient Heshbon, not far from Amman, capital
of present day Jordan. The water in them would be still, clear and
deep; an apt picture of healthy, love-filled eyes. The gate of Bath-
rabbim was probably the name of one of the gates into the city of
Heshbon. Since, however, "Bath-rabbim" means in Hebrew
"daughter of many", there is some justification for the New
English Bible's translation, "the crowded city". If the description
of her eyes seems apt, what are we to make of the picture of her
nose as being "like a tower of Lebanon, overlooking Damascus"
(v. 4)? Since the tower of Lebanon probably refers to the
Lebanon mountain massif which rises to over 9000 feet, this
seems a somewhat exaggerated compliment even if large noses
were in biblical times, considered a sign of beauty—a view for
which there is scant evidence. It may be that her nose, although
not unduly large, was strikingly beautiful and seemed to domi-
nate her face, as the Lebanon mountains towered over
Damascus. The word "Lebanon", however, is similar in sound to
the Hebrew words for 'whiteness' and 'frankincense', so there
might just be a reference to the colour of her nose or its fragrance:

compare 5:13 where the lover's cheeks are described as being "beds of spices". So, finally in verse 5, her head as a whole. It crowns her body, as the Mount Carmel range dominates the coastal plain of Palestine. Her hair cascades down in long flowing tresses with their dark purple sheen, beautiful enough to captivate a king (see 1:4). There is an Egyptian love poem in which the man confesses:

> With her hair she lassoes me,
> with her eyes she pulls me in.

(d) 7:6–9*a*: Certainly this man is well and truly caught. While others may use fulsome and evocative words to describe the beauty of the girl in his life, their words are the dispassionate words of the onlooker. Not so his. She is not only in his eyes "fair" or "beautiful"—a word he has used frequently from 1:8 onwards—and "pleasant" or "gracious", she is 'love [rather than "loved one"] with delights', or with a slight alteration of the text, "daughter of delights" (NEB). The RSV "O loved one, delectable maiden" reads well, but hardly catches the full meaning of the words. Both "love" and "delights" have a sexual flavour: for him she represents all the delights associated with love-making. So he depicts her as a stately palm tree, her breasts the clusters of dates. He must climb the tree to harvest them and taste their sweetness. The picture then changes from the date palm to the vine (v. 8*b*), with her breasts now the ripe bunches of grapes, and "the scent of [her] breath", or perhaps her nipples, being compared to apples or apricots (see comment on 2:3). Her kisses (v. 9*a*, literally 'your palate or mouth') are like the most delectable wine; this is a compliment that she had already bestowed on him in 5:16.

The rest of verse 9 raises serious difficulties of interpretation, but unless the text is altered it is probably best taken (see GNB, JB, NIV) as the point at which the woman breaks into her lover's words, picks up his picture of the wine of love, and says to him, 'Yes, let it glide down smoothly, dripping on the lips of those who are asleep,' or, following the Greek text, dripping on lips and teeth, a reading followed in most modern translations. Either way the words indicate her eager response to her lover's reaching out with desire for her.

LET ALL THE WORLD KNOW!

Song of Solomon 7:10–8:4

> [10]I am my beloved's,
>> and his desire is for me.
> [11]Come, my beloved,
>> let us go forth into the fields,
>> and lodge in the villages;
> [12]let us go out early to the vineyards,
>> and see whether the vines have budded,
>> whether the grape blossoms have opened
>> and the pomegranates are in bloom.
>> There I will give you my love.
> [13]The mandrakes give forth fragrance,
>> and over our doors are all choice fruits,
>> new as well as old,
>>> which I have laid up for you, O my beloved.

> [1]O that you were like a brother to me,
>> that nursed at my mother's breast!
> If I met you outside, I would kiss you,
>> and none would despise me.
> [2]I would lead you and bring you
>> into the house of my mother,
>> and into the chamber of her that conceived me.
> I would give you spiced wine to drink,
>> the juice of my pomegranates.
> [3]O that his left hand were under my head,
>> and that his right hand embraced me!
> [4]I adjure you, O daughters of Jerusalem,
>> that you stir not up nor awaken love
>> until it please.

Following her eager wish in verse 9*b*, the woman responds openly and unashamedly to her lover's advances. She belongs to him "and his desire is for me" (v. 10). The only other place in the Old Testament where this word "desire" is found is in Genesis 3:16 where, as part of her penalty for disobeying God, Eve is told:

> Your desire shall be for your husband,
>> and he shall rule over you.

That desire in Genesis is something imposed upon Eve, and indicates her submission: here it expresses the joyful claim that links man and woman, each to the other. She thinks of his desire not as domination, but as shared joy. It may be that as in the case of Ecclesiastes (see p. 24) a motif taken from earlier biblical material is being deliberately used with a different meaning.

Now she is ready to accept the invitation that she dreamt he gave her in 2:10ff. Come, she says, let us go out into the fields, seeking the solitude love desires; let us "lodge in the villages" (v. 11) or better, as in the New English Bible, let us "lie among the henna bushes", a plant native to Palestine which produces clusters of sweet smelling yellow and white flowers. Even one villager would have been one too many for these lovers! Eagerly, using the familiar picture of the garden with its various plants (see comment on 4:12), she declares that she will be ripe for love. The only other reference to "mandrakes" (verse 7:13) in the Old Testament is to be found in Genesis 30:14–16 where Leah's son brings her mandrakes so that she may bear another child to Jacob. The mandrake plant was supposed to have all kinds of potent powers, including that of being an aphrodisiac—compare John Donne's lines from his poem:

> Goe and catche a falling starre,
> Get with childe a mandrake roote.

She is ready for love. She has much to teach him, "new as well as old" (v. 13). Whatever she may have given him in the past, there are new realms of love waiting to be explored.

She has one regret. To be alone in his arms out there in the countryside is pleasure enough, but she longs for the day when she may openly profess that love so that all the world will know of it. Their love for one another may be intensely private, but it longs for public recognition, as all true love does. It may mature in secrecy, but it desires to be shared with others. It is quite likely that the lovers are as yet neither betrothed nor married. She wishes that she could openly express her affection for him, when-ever she meets or finds him, as a sister may publicly express her affection for a brother (8:1). She wishes that she could take him home to her mother's house, "and into the chamber of her that conceived me" (8:2). This rendering assumes an alteration of the text to bring it into line with 3:4 (see comment there). It is a reasonable alteration, but not strictly necessary. The Hebrew text as it stands can be translated in one of two ways: (1) 'into the house of my mother who taught me', the mother who instructed her as a child and perhaps more specifically taught her the facts of life, and (2) 'into the house of my mother where you will teach me', in which case she is expressing the hope that her lover will instruct her more fully in the art of making love in the very place where she first experienced love from her mother. The first is more likely since throughout 8:1–2 the emphasis is on the initiative of the woman. Not only the place, but the mood must be right. She will supply him with "spiced [or mulled] wine" (v. 2)—a word that occurs only here in the Old Testament, but probably indicates some exotic mixed drink—and pomegranate juice (4:13).

Chapter 8 verses 3–4 repeat 2:6–7 (see comment there). There is no longer, however, any reference to "the gazelles or the hinds of the field", and the form of the concluding words is subtly different, although this is not indicated in most of the English translations. Whereas in 2:7 and 3:5 they are in the form of an oath, "[I adjure you] . . . that you stir not up or awaken . . . ", here they open with an oath, 'What or why should you stir . . . ?" There is no longer any need to plead that their love be allowed to take its natural course. Once she has brought him home and their relationship is there for all the world to acknowledge, she defies anyone to interfere.

THE GREATEST OF THESE IS LOVE

Song of Solomon 8:5–7

> [5]Who is that coming up from the wilderness,
>   leaning upon her beloved?
>
> Under the apple tree I awakened you.
> There your mother was in travail with you,

there she who bore you was in travail.
⁶Set me as a seal upon your heart,
    as a seal upon your arm;
for love is strong as death,
    jealousy is cruel as the grave,
Its flashes are flashes of fire,
    a most vehement flame.
⁷Many waters cannot quench love,
    neither can floods drown it.
If a man offered for love
    all the wealth of his house,
    it would be utterly scorned.

The rest of the book, particularly from 8:8ff., has been the subject of endless debate. Many wish to end the book with this section. You will find in the Jerusalem Bible, for example, that 8:8ff. is regarded as a series of appendices, and an attempt is made to find an appropriate background for the appendices, an attempt more ingenious than convincing. The view taken here is that from 8:5ff. we are witnessing something like the curtain call at the end of a play or musical. One by one the leading characters come forward, take a bow, and through a characteristic action or by a few well chosen words, recall what has gone before.

First of all, in verse 5*a*, the companions, the daughters of Jerusalem, introduce the couple by echoing the question which we have heard earlier in this book: "Who is that coming up from the wilderness . . . ?" (see comment on 3:6). The word translated "leaning" occurs only here in the Old Testament; the Good News Bible's rendering "arm in arm with her lover" neatly conveys the required meaning.

The girl, however, who speaks in verses 5*b*–7 has no time for any further conversation with her companions; her thoughts are concentrated solely on her lover and on the matchless love that unites them. She imagines herself (v. 5*b*) gently awakening him as they lie together under the apple or apricot tree, to share their love in the very place where his mother conceived him or gave birth to him—the Hebrew word translated "was in travail" could mean either of these. What incident if any lies behind these words, we do not know—she is not, as in 8:2, speaking of her own mother—but the girl regards it as fitting that in the place where life first came to her lover, they should be thus celebrating and ultimately creating new life.

She then (vv. 6–7), speaks of their love in words which, in many respects, may claim to mark the climax of the book. In the ancient world, people of standing had their own personal seal, with which they stamped documents or property. It was like a personal signature or a Banker's card. Such seals were worn either attached to a cord around the neck (Gen. 38:18) or as a ring on the finger (Jer. 22:24)— the word translated "arm" in verse 6 should probably be taken to mean 'hand' or 'finger'. Such a seal was nothing if not personal property; so this girl longs to be as close to him, as much a part of him as his seal. As so often, profound thoughts can centre upon simple things like this seal, and something of little value in itself can carry a rich world of meaning. Nowhere is this more finely expressed than in George Crabbe's words about his mother's wedding ring:

> The ring so worn, as you behold,
> So thin, so pale, is yet of gold:
> The passion such it was to prove:
> Worn with life's cares, love yet was love.

Such love she declares is as "strong", as irresistible, as inescapable, as death itself: such "jealousy" or rather such passion and the exclusive claims it makes, is as "cruel", as hard and unyielding as "the grave", Hebrew *sheol*, the shadowy world of the dead (see comment on Eccles. 3:20). Only when we remember the chill, negative inevitability of death and *sheol* in Hebrew thinking, can we appreciate the tremendous claim that is here being made for love. Love stands as the one truly creative and constructive force which throws down the gauntlet and defies the destructive forces in experience.

The power of such love is underlined in two phrases at the end of verse 6. (1) "Its flashes are flashes of fire": the word here translated "flashes" can mean arrows (Ps. 76:3). The Hebrew word (*reshep*) may have some connection with the Canaanite god Reshep, god of war and pestilence, sometimes called "lord of the arrow". What now flashes across the sky, heading for their target with deadly effect are the fiery arrows or darts of love, an image which is to be developed on the basis of classical literature in terms of the fiery shafts and bolts of Cupid. And (2) "a most vehement flame"; behind this lies one Hebrew word which has caused a good deal of discussion. It is possible to divide it so that it can be translated, "the flame of the Lord" (cf. JB), which would be a way of talking about the consuming love of God. It is highly unlikely, however, that there should be but one cryptic reference to God in the entire book. Both the RSV and the New International Version take "the Lord" metaphorically as expressing a powerful or superlative idea: thus the New International Version has "a mighty flame". Without being divided, the word might mean 'lightning itself', a further description of the flashing, fiery darts of the previous phrase.

Such powerful love is also (v. 7) indestructible. The "many [or mighty] waters" and "the floods" may be an echo of the threatening powers of chaos which in ancient Near Eastern mythology had to be quelled to bring creation into being and were always a potential threat to the God-ordered life of the world. The association of such 'mighty waters' with death and destruction is vividly illustrated in Psalm 18, where the Psalmist describes the crisis in his life in the following terms:

> When the bonds of death held me fast,
>   destructive torrents overtook me,
> the bonds of Sheol tightened round me,
>   the snares of death were set to catch me;

(vv. 4–5, NEB)

He then describes God coming to deliver him:

> He reached down from the height and took me,
>   he drew me out of the mighty waters . . . .

(v. 16, NEB)

Defiantly, against all that may be dark or threatening in life, this girl throws into the balance the inextinguishable flame of love.

Nor can such love be bought (v. 7*b*). Anyone who tries to do so will soon find that even if he offered all the wealth that he possessed, "it would be utterly scorned", or as the Good News Bible translates, "contempt is all he would get" (the subject of the last line being either "it", the wealth of his house, or he himself, the man who possesses "it"). There are things in life for which you cannot write a blank cheque; there are riches that money cannot buy, and high on that list is love.

ALL'S WELL THAT ENDS WELL

Song of Solomon 8:8–14

8We have a little sister,
   and she has no breasts.
What shall we do for our sister,
   on the day when she is spoken for?
9If she is a wall,
   we will build upon her a battlement of silver;
   but if she is a door,
   we will enclose her with boards of cedar.
10I was a wall,
   and my breasts were like towers;
then I was in his eyes
   as one who brings peace.

11Solomon had a vineyard at Baal-hamon;
   he let out the vineyard to keepers;
   each one was to bring for its fruit a thousand pieces of silver.
12My vineyard, my very own, is for myself;
   you, O Solomon, may have the thousand,
   and the keepers of the fruit two hundred.

13O you who dwell in the gardens,
   my companions are listening for your voice;
   let me hear it.

¹⁴Make haste, my beloved,
    and be like a gazelle
  or a young stag
    upon the mountains of spices.

This closing section of the book contains three elements:

(a) Verses 8–10: a dialogue, probably between the girl and her brothers;

(b) Verses 11–12: the man speaks about the precious treasure he has found in his beloved; and

(c) Verses 13–14: a brief concluding *pas de deux* from the two lovers.

(a) As we have seen earlier (1:6) the girl's brothers were not exactly sympathetic to her blossoming romance. Since they were responsible for arranging marriage for their younger sister, they here express their doubts as to whether she is yet ready for marriage. What are they to say when someone asks for her hand in marriage? In their eyes she is not yet sexually mature, "she has no breasts" (v. 8). But what do they then mean by describing her as a "wall" or "a door" (v. 9)? It may be argued that the wall and the door are to be taken as opposites, the strong wall indicating her chastity which they will vigorously protect, the door which opens indicating promiscuity, which they will take steps to thwart, boarding it up with strong cedar planks. But a door is also there to bar entry into a house, and both wall and door may point to her chastity or strength of character. No-one is going to be allowed to play around with their little sister.

The girl then picks up their words (v. 10). 'Yes', she says 'I am a wall'—not "I was" as in RSV—'but I *am* ready for love and marriage'. She describes her well-formed breasts as being like towers on this wall. Not only that, but she knows to whom she wishes to give herself, one in whose presence she finds peace or fulfilment (Hebrew *shalom*, a word that always points to completeness or fullness of life). In such circumstances we must assume that the brothers would withdraw their objections.

(b) Solomon may not have a leading role to play in the Song that bears his name in English Bibles, although not in the

Hebrew, but he is now used by the man as an example of someone who, in spite of all that he possesses, is not in the least to be envied. Solomon may have a vineyard in Baal-hamon (v. 11), in all probability a place name although attempts to identify it have not been very successful (unless it be the northern district of Hammon referred to in Joshua 19:28); he may let it out to tenant farmers for a rental of a thousand pieces of silver. If the going rate indicated in Isaiah 7:23—"a thousand vines, worth a thousand shekels of silver"—still held good when this poem was written, then it must have been a very large vineyard with huge numbers of vines. Let it out, the lover says to Solomon, get your rental, let the tenant farmers get their more modest return (two hundred pieces of silver as opposed to Solomon's one thousand per plot): I don't care; I have one "vineyard" and it's my very own.

There may, however, be another level on which we should interpret these verses. We have already seen (1:6) the way in which the vineyard is used as a symbol for the girl herself and her sexuality—and undoubtedly that is meant here—but the word "Baal-hamon" could mean 'lord of a crowd' or 'husband of a crowd'. Is there a dig here at Solomon with his "seven hundred wives" and "three hundred concubines" (1 Kings 11:3)? He had so many women whom he could only use as objects to gratify his sexual desires or whom he could loan out to others for a similar purpose. Over and against such debasement which treats women as sexual objects or property, this lover places his exclusive one-to-one relationship with his beloved as an example of what love really means. Certainly this book as a whole gives no support to those who would wish to trivialize sex or divorce it from that total relationship of which, at its most wholesome, it is an expression.

(c) In a brief final *pas de deux*, the lover calls upon his beloved to respond to his presence. He claims that both he and his companions are listening attentively to catch the sound of her voice (v. 13). She responds immediately in words which echo many of the pictures of love that have appeared earlier in this book. She invites him to come quickly into her arms, there to savour the joys of love. For the picture of the gazelle and the young stag, see the comment on 2:17; for the mountains of spice, see the comment on 4:6.

IN RETROSPECT

There we must leave our "pair of star-cross'd lovers". Let us now return to the question we left hanging in the air in the Introduction: what purpose does this book serve in that collection of sacred writings which we call the Bible? If you have been increasingly puzzled by this question, this may have as much to say about you and your view of religion as it has to say about the Bible. Let me suggest two things that are worth pondering:

(1) Let us consider first an issue to which attention has been drawn on more than one occasion in the course of the commentary, for it is worth underlining. An old Jewish tailor, in the course of a serious conversation with a Christian friend, once said, "The real difference between the Jewish and the Christian religion is that we Jews believe in sex!" He had a point. From an early period in the history of the Church, thanks largely to a false separation of body and spirit, sex tended to be regarded with suspicion or as being appropriate for those whose footsteps were only on the lower rungs of the ladder of spirituality. Not surprisingly, against this background, an allegorical approach which sought to spiritualize the Song of Solomon flourished. What else could you do with the book? The book is, however, from beginning to end, a liberating celebration of human sexuality as something which is good and holy, something not merely functional, but to be enjoyed, something not merely casual, but totally self-giving and demanding, something that makes of two people "one flesh" (Gen. 2:24) and joins them together in a relationship which colours all that they do and are.

A Christian ethic of sex goes sadly astray unless it begins here. In the Song of Solomon there is no trivializing of sexuality, only a joyful acceptance of it as one of the most powerful forces in human experience. There are no snide innuendos, no crude jokes, for a reason which was well put by William Temple: "The reason for not joking about sex is exactly the same as for not joking about the Holy Communion. It is not that the subject is nasty, but that it is sacred, and to joke about it is profanity".

The false asceticism of a previous age would have done well to listen to the Song of Solomon instead of taking refuge in allegorizing it; the perverted and often trivialized sexuality of our own times could find it an equally challenging corrective.

(2) Without resorting to allegory or to any detailed typological interpretation let us remember that the language the Bible uses about God is language drawn by analogy from our human experience, our human activities, our human emotions. There is no other language we can use, although the Old Testament is aware that there are limitations to the way in which human feelings and activities may be ascribed to God. He is, to quote Hosea's words, "God and not man, the Holy One in your midst" (Hos. 11:9). Nevertheless when we use such language and apply it to God, it must have some links with the human experience which lies behind the words we use. There is no point, for example, in calling God 'good' if God's goodness is something entirely different from what we understand by the word 'good'. So is it with the word 'love'.

Sometimes a very sharp distinction has been drawn between different kinds of love: the human love which has the element of sexuality in it (Greek *eros*) and disinterested love (Greek *agape*) which provides the model for God's love. It is a distinction which can be pushed too far. There is an interesting passage in Deuteronomy 7:7–8 which is trying to explain the mystery of God's choice of Israel and his people:

> It was not because you were more in number than any other people that the Lord set his love upon you and chose you, for you were the fewest of all peoples; but it is because the Lord loves you, and is keeping the oath which he swore to your fathers . . . .

What this RSV translation conceals is that behind the words "set his love upon you" and "loves you" there are two different Hebrew words. The *first* one, rendered "set his love upon you", is not a very common word in the Old Testament, but where it does occur elsewhere it has strongly sexual connotations or at least points to a desire aroused by something of value in the object of desire. The *second* word, rendered "loves you", is a common word used for many kinds of human relationships: parents and children, husband and wife, for example. If Deuteronomy can use both of these words in its effort to explain the mystery of God's relationship with Israel, it must be because what love means in human relationships provides us with a clue to what the love of God means.

So too with the New Testament affirmation that "God so loved the world that he gave his only Son" (John 3:16). As we explore the mystery of human love and come face to face in the Song of Solomon with the total and tender self giving of the lovers to each other, we shall be reminded of the depth and mystery of God's self-giving love for the world, and also of the responsive love to which he calls us (1 John 4:7–10).

When we come to the climax of the book with its assertion (8:6–7): "Love is strong as death—Many waters cannot quench love, neither can floods drown it", we can hear through these words the claim of the Gospel that the love of God, incarnate in Jesus, is the one reality that nothing can destroy, and we are challenged to live our lives in that faith. It is not only as strong as death, but stronger. The love that faced death on the cross, rose in triumph. Using the same kind of nature imagery which we have found in the Song of Solomon, an Easter hymn declares:

> Forth he came at Easter like the risen grain,
> He that for three days in the grave had lain;
> Quick from the dead my Risen Lord is seen:
> > Love is come again,
> > Like wheat that springeth green.

In reliving the human love relationship which the Song of Solomon celebrates—its totality, its holiness, its power—we are being pointed to that greater relationship in the light of which we can say, "... we are more than conquerors through him who loved us. For I am sure that neither death, nor life, nor angels, nor principalities, nor things present, nor things to come, nor powers, nor height, nor depth, nor anything else in all creation, will be able to separate us from the love of God in Christ Jesus our Lord" (Rom. 8:37–38).

It is part of the unfailing fascination of the Old Testament that it places side by side two such different books as Ecclesiastes and Song of Solomon:

The one shrewdly, almost coldly intellectual, the other warm, suffused with the language of the heart;

The one sadly cynical about women, the other in which a woman plays the leading role in the dialogue of love;

The one haunted by the chill destructiveness of death, the other affirming that love is as strong as death;

The one perplexed as to whether life has any discernible meaning, the other finding meaning in the most intimate of all human relationships.

It is witness to the richness of the Bible that this should be so, a richness to which we shall be blind if we come to the Bible insisting that there must be one simple message running through it from beginning to end.

FURTHER READING

The books marked with an asterisk are suitable as an introduction to the study of Ecclesiastes and Song of Solomon.

Many commentaries deal with both books, sometimes in conjunction with others:

* W. J. Fuerst, *The Book of Ruth, Esther, Ecclesiastes, Song of Songs, Lamentations* (Cambridge University Press, 1975)
C. D. Ginsburg, *The Song of Songs and Coheleth* (Ktav, New York, 1970) (a reprint of two volumes originally published separately in the 19th Century)

ECCLESIASTES

* M. A. Eaton, *Ecclesiastes, an Introduction and Commentary* (Inter-Varsity Press, Leicester, 1983)
R. Gordis, *Koheleth, the Man and his World* (Ktav, New York, 1955)
* E. Jones, *Proverbs, Ecclesiastes* (SCM Press, 1961)
* D. Kidner, *The Message of Ecclesiastes* (The Bible Speaks Today; Inter-Varsity Press, Leicester, 1976)
R. B. Y. Scott, *Proverbs, Ecclesiastes* (The Anchor Bible, New York, 1965)

SONG OF SOLOMON

M. V. Fox, *The Song of Songs and the Ancient Egyptian Love Songs* (University of Wisconsin Press, London, 1985)
R. Gordis, *The Song of Songs* (Ktav, New York, 1968)
* G. A. F. Knight, *Song of Songs* (SCM Press, 1955)

* G. Lloyd Carr, *The Song of Solomon* (Inter-Varsity Press, Leicester, 1984)

M. H. Pope, *Song of Songs* (The Anchor Bible, New York, 1977)

H. H. Rowley, "The Interpretation of the Song of Songs" in *The Servant of the Lord and other Essays on the Old Testament* (Blackwell, Oxford, 1965)